Imaginative Events
for Training

Imaginative Events
for Training

A Trainer's Sourcebook of Games,
Simulations, and Role-Play Exercises

Ken Jones

McGRAW-HILL, INC.

New York   San Francisco   Washington, D.C.   Auckland   Bogotá
Caracas   Lisbon   London   Madrid   Mexico City   Milan
Montreal   New Delhi   San Juan   Singapore
Sydney   Tokyo   Toronto

The sponsoring editor for this book was Karen Hansen, the editing supervisor was Jane Palmieri, and the production supervisor was Suzanne W. Babeuf. Designed, arranged, and typeset by Ken Jones.

Printed and bound by Malloy Lithographing, Inc.

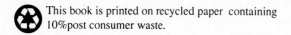 This book is printed on recycled paper containing 10%post consumer waste.

HD30.26.J655 1993

Contents

Acknowledgements   vii

Introduction   1

Overview   3
Descriptions of the events   5
Skills and other forms of behaviour   11
Introducing the events   15
Running the events   17
Running the debriefing   19
In defence of the imaginative   21

Creativity areas   23

1 Banana peel   25
2 Executess   31
3 Historical words   36
4 Marbledown   40
5 Singing refrigerator   48
6 Tax image   53
7 The Trap   58
8 Weldo Junction   65

Efficiency areas   69

 9 Designing soap   71
10 Disharmony activator   80
11 Escape   83
12 Fold here   94
13 Houses challenge   102
14 Into Green and Care   108
15 Number auction   116
16 Whistlers and movers   120

Personal areas   125

17 Afterwards   127
18 Cosmetic friends   131
19 Gene people   136
20 Human zoo   140
21 Leaks   146
22 Romantic dream   151
23 Sorcerer's apprentice   155
24 To the courts   158

Creativity areas 165

25 Creating portraits 167
26 Empty boxes lecture 173
27 Ghost stories 178
28 Hyp-hen 183
29 Levitation pill 187
30 Ministries of labels 194
31 Real real 199
32 Rollercoaster 205

Efficiency areas 211

33 Anagram scores 213
34 Eliminating words 218
35 Fungus 225
36 Gender in law 230
37 Helpers 233
38 Sports edition 240
39 Trading values 246
40 Women managers 256

Personal areas 261

41 Assortment of clerks 263
42 Born today 269
43 Doppelgangers and mirrors 275
44 Health machine 281
45 Management philosophy 287
46 Missing disc 290
47 Prison prospects 297
48 Same Again Wine Co. 307

Acknowledgements

Most events for education and training need to be tested out as they depend on people's behaviour, which can be unpredictable. Testing requires willing volunteers and so it is to the hundreds of students, trainees, instructors and teachers that I owe the profoundest debt of gratitude. Apart from actually running the events I find it extremely valuable to 'walk the course' with people who have often run interactive events and who can point out potential snags and difficulties.

I am particularly indebted to friends in SAGSET – the main UK society in the field of active learning events – and its international equivalent ISAGA. Internationally I have received considerable help from teachers and trainers in Denmark, Germany, France, Japan and the United States.

For individual events in Part 1 I thank Danny Saunders, the Editor of SAGSET's journal *Simulation – Games for Learning* for mentioning the outline of an idea I used for Whistlers and movers – if I remember rightly the original was about sheep and only one shepherd whistled at a time.

For individual events in Part 2 I thank several knowledgeable friends in the field of art and science for discussing Creating portraits and the Levitation pill.

In designing and typesetting this book I used an Acorn Archimedes A3000 computer with Computer Concept's Impression II, a document processor. The printer was LaserDirect, also by Computer Concepts.

Imaginative Events for Training

Introduction

Overview

There are two parts to this book. Both have the same format, the same number of events and the same categories. They are different only in their contents. The events in the two parts – simulations, exercises, puzzles, games – all have the same objectives. They are all intended to:

* jog minds and challenge routine ideas
* encourage innovative thinking
* help participants learn how to cope with change
* provoke and amuse.

I have tried to achieve these aims by devising somewhat unusual situations in which success depends upon thinking rather than memory. I wanted to get away from most other books of events that place heavy emphasis on the aims and objectives of the facilitator and make large claims about what learning will be achieved, but the events themselves are often empty structures or have factual details which replicate reality to the point of dullness. Their authors' stress on learning answers rather than exploring questions conveys the impression that the events are just instructional methodology in a new guise.

Although my other books also contain imaginative activities, in this book I group events under areas of thought and behaviour so that facilitators (trainers, teachers, tutors) can find their way around the diverse offerings. By 'areas' I do not mean subjects (politics, business) or skills (diplomacy, team building) or controversies (the environment, drug abuse). 'Areas' relate to what the participants actually think and do. This is different to most books, which categorize events into 'objectives'. By definition, an objective is not something that happens, it is an aim.

I use three broad categories of thought and behaviour:

* creativity areas
* efficiency areas
* personal areas.

I list them in alphabetical order – they have no order of importance. The idea is that the facilitator looks for areas of thought and behaviour that match the situation. For example, a personnel manager running a course might wish to explore the personal areas, while the organizer of a conference on environmental problems might look at events in both the personal and the efficiency categories. A course involving media matters could concentrate on the creativity area. Teachers and trainers who have problems with bored students might look at the events in all three areas.

Creativity areas of thought and behaviour

By creativity areas I mean the thoughts and behaviour involved in producing something new, as distinct from a rearrangement. If a company (person, institution) does procedure X followed by procedure Y, then it would be an innovative rearrangement to do Y before X, whereas it would be creative to devise procedure Z, even though Z might never be used.

Efficiency areas of thought and behaviour

I see efficiency areas as consisting of organizational thoughts and behaviour. It does not exclude personal or creative considerations, but it is the attitudes of mind that occur when a person is engaged in management. By management I do not mean a group of people in the boardroom. I use management as an action word related to what people think and do when they manage – whether they are in charge of a multinational company or cooking dinner.

Personal areas of thought and behaviour

Personal areas embrace the thoughts about oneself and others as human beings, as distinct from human resources. It includes one's own ethics, attitudes, beliefs, emotions, artistry, sympathy, competitiveness, selfishness, compassion, understanding.

Descriptions of the events

To help choose suitable events, here are brief summaries of the events in this book.

Creativity areas

1 Banana peel

In this simulation the participants are asked to invent a banana peeler and advertise it. It can be either a fun product or one that actually works.

2 Executess

A simulation in which editorial staff of the new international women's business magazine *Executess* are asked to draw up a consistent house style that identifies gender.

3 Historical words

A simulation about presentations to rehabilitate core words.

4 Marbledown

A simulation in which teams have to build a device made of paper and paper-clips that brings a marble down from a height to a located position and then present and demonstrate their device.

5 Singing refrigerator

A simulation about managers in four departments of a white goods manufacturing company who have to draw up a five-question questionnaire about the marketing potential of a singing refrigerator.

6 Tax image

A simulation in which executives of an advertising company deal with a request from a Third-World oil-producing country for a campaign to make the paying of taxes less unpopular.

7 The Trap

A simulation about a restaurant chain that has commissioned four experts dealing with advertising, decor, logo and restaurant layout to produce a feasibility study for a restaurant called The Trap.

8 Weldo Junction

A simulation about a plan by the City Council of Weldo Junction to attract visitors to the city – a city that outsiders regard as a joke.

Efficiency areas

9 Designing soap

A simulation about a television company having separate meetings with three production companies about their proposals to produce a new soap opera. This event has a hidden agenda.

10 Disharmony activator

This is a simulation in which an inventor has offered an electronic manufacturing company a device to register disharmonies between people and give advice. The company has to decide whether or not to accept the terms proposed by the inventor and how to market the device.

11 Escape

A simulation in which failure to escape from the labyrinth means death to the whole team, even though failure may have been due to lack of cooperation from one of its members.

12 Fold here

This is a simulation in which groups are asked to take part in an exercise in which they have to follow instructions involving documents relating to the construction of a model tower out of paper and paper-clips.

13 Houses challenge

A game in which the Lords and Ladies of the Houses of Stone, Paper and Scissors can challenge each other, but first have to identify not only the other two houses, but also their own. Each player is given a name tag plus a clue. This event can be run in the format of an icebreaker.

14 Into Green and Care

A simulation about a woman who has inherited her late husband's business and has decided to manage it with the help of her family. This event has a hidden agenda.

15 Number auction

An exercise in which 4 teams, each with 14 dollars, take part in an auction of 5 numbers. The numbers are later valued according to given specifications.

16 Whistlers and movers

A simulation in which three teams, each containing a Whistler and several Movers, have the job of guiding blindfolded Movers into a particular part of the room, the event taking place at the Selection and Training Centre of Naval Intelligence.

17 Afterwards

In this simulation, the participants have the roles of four managers dealing with hypotheticals, strategies, positives and negatives and tackle the problem of how the lessons of the course could be applied back at work.

18 Cosmetic friends

This is a simulation of the management of a cosmetics company in which it is discovered that the reason behind the recent spate of disruptive short-term office romances is the aphrodisiac effect of the recently introduced colour decor.

19 Gene people

The Gene people is a simulation about Parano, a country with a minority race of above average intelligence. This situation has resulted in racial discrimination.

20 Human zoo

A simulation set in the future in which rulers of Africa, America, Asia, Europe and the Middle East are faced with the problem of space travellers who have arrived with the object of studying the dominant life form on earth and request the building of a human zoo to enable them to do this without causing general disruption to life on the planet.

21 Leaks

A simulation in which the senior members of the Government of Alpha inquire into a serious leak of information to the media. This event has a hidden agenda.

22 Romantic dream

This is a simulation of an author's dream in which the participants are six job descriptions in search of their gender and character in an unwritten romantic novel in which the main character must be a woman but must not be the secretary. This event can be run in the format of an icebreaker.

23 Sorcerer's apprentice

This is a simulation of interviews by sorcerers (or sorceresses) seeking apprentices. This event can be run in the format of an icebreaker.

24 To the courts

A simulation about a civil claim for compensation by a home owner whose fence has been damaged by a car owner. Both sides have legal advisers and have the choice of an out-of-court settlement or a court action in which they can be represented by either a top, expensive lawyer or an average, less expensive lawyer.

Creativity areas

25 Creating portraits

This is a simulation in which artists and patrons create portraits in a step-by-step manner, changing roles halfway through each meeting. It can be run in the format of an icebreaker.

26 Empty boxes lecture

A simulation in which college staff have to prepare a lecture on counselling, having only the diagram of empty boxes and arrows produced by the lecturer who was to take the class but is ill.

27 Ghost stories

A simulation in which participants are eighteenth-century writers describing a ghost and later twentieth-century hotel owners trying to make use of the alleged ghost for publicity purposes.

28 Hyp-hen

This is a simulation of a group test for applicants for the job of creative writers to Media Comedy Enterprises. They have to insert hyphens in words and redefine the meanings accordingly.

29 Levitation pill

A simulation to prepare a secret report for the Government of Alpha on the possible consequences of releasing the levitation pill.

30 Ministries of labels

In this simulation, participants are in charge of four ministries in the Government of Alpha that have been requested to state what they actually do in order to see whether money can be saved. The ministries can negotiate with each other.

31 Real real

This is a simulation about planning a quest for the real real.

32 Rollercoaster

A simulation in which teams design and build the last section of a paper rollercoaster.

33 Anagram scores

An exercise in which players have to prepare for three minutes of action during which they try to form words from nine letters. Each team chooses one of three groups of letters during its preparation and the scores depend not on the number or length of the words, but on how many prechosen letters they contain.

34 Eliminating words

This simulation is about a feasibility study in the Kingdom of Lexicona aimed at eliminating inessential words from the vocabulary used for public communications.

35 Fungus

A simulation in which managers of a large supermarket have to deal with the problem of a fungus that appears to grow on the working surfaces of computers.

36 Gender in law

A simulation set in the Republic of Delta, where a private investigation by the largest law firm has produced some unexpected evidence regarding the way juries behave in relation to gender.

37 Helpers

A simulation involving trainee counsellors at the Government's Health at Work Agency who take on the roles of managers, workers and counsellors in construction tasks using paper. This simulation has a hidden agenda.

38 Sports edition

A simulation set in the Republic of Remote where the population of the villages are keen to buy the sports edition of whichever of the two local newspapers delivers first. Each newspaper has two delivery trucks, both owned independently, and the owners are paid according to the number of sales. Within each newspaper the truck owners can negotiate their routes between themselves.

39 Trading values

A game that starts with each player ranking five symbols in order of personal value. Players meet in pairs and symbols are traded on a one-to-one basis. The official value of individual symbols can be fixed by agreement.

40 Women managers

A simulation about the executors of a large trust who are seeking to promote, enhance and improve the status of women in business and management.

41 Assortment of clerks

A simulation about a large organization that has to make cuts in clerical staff because of the introduction of a computer system. The event has a hidden agenda – all the clerks are made redundant in their second interview.

42 Born today

Babies with at least 70 years of life expectancy meet professional counsellors and professional trainers. The event can be run in the format of an icebreaker.

43 Doppelgangers and mirrors

A simulation set in the Misty World of Identity in which the participants are imaginary persons facing some problem of identity who meet doppelgangers or mirrors who advise them.

44 Health machine

This is a simulation in which managers of the Centrum Hospital of the Republic of Alpha discuss what to do with an interplanetary health machine.

45 Management philosophy

A simulation involving a country where employers have been divided into different groups according to their managerial philosophy. Counsellors interview job seekers to see if their philosophies are compatible with those of a potential employer. The simulation could be run in the format of an icebreaker.

46 Missing disc

A simulation in which the Security Manager of a computer software company interviews three other managers, one of whom might have been responsible for the disappearance of a valuable confidential computer program.

47 Prison prospects

This is a simulation about new prisoners, gang leaders and senior warders.

48 Same Again Wine Co.

A simulation about a wine company that recruited staff on the basis of compatibility with existing members of staff and, as a result, has potential problems regarding race and gender.

Skills and other forms of behaviour

In addition to categorizing events according to areas of the mind, I have followed the traditional practice of setting down the facilitator's objectives in terms of skills.

A look at other books in this field suggests that most authors are unclear about skill categories. They do not explain what the labels mean and often seem to use them interchangeably. The following examples may clarify the categories of skill and behaviour, and the distinctions could be useful when assessing and debriefing the events.

Categories

Communication

By this I mean not *what* is communicated but *how* it is communicated – how people think, talk, listen and put forward ideas. It covers body language as well as spoken language and involves both common sense and logic. It is probably the broadest of the skill categories.

Counselling

This is a situation in which people need help on a personal (albeit hypothetical) level from someone who can try to sympathize, understand and advise. It means active counselling, not simply planning to counsel.

Diplomacy

The meaning does not relate to professional diplomacy as such, but is used instead in the sense in which one person might say to another, 'You could have been more diplomatic'. Diplomacy is usually a high-order skill, involving understanding other people's needs. It can be deceitful and it can be competitive, but it need be neither.

Gender and race

Although not skills, these are extremely important areas of behaviour. The categories also serve as signposts marked 'Opportunities, but danger of exposed sensitivities'.

Hidden agenda

Although not a skill, it is, like gender and race, a warning that temperatures can rise. People can become upset. However, some of the most powerful and effective events do have hidden agendas.

Icebreaker

Icebreakers are suitable not only at the beginning of courses but at any point when 'ice' has formed – when there are frosty silences or when the participants have frozen themselves into groups based on sex or race or job. The format of an icebreaker is to provide an opportunity for each participant to meet as many other participants as reasonably possible in the time available.

Negotiation

Unlike diplomacy, negotiation necessarily involves bargaining. Usually what is at issue is fairly clear cut, such as goods, services and money.

Planning

By planning I do not mean the plan itself, I mean the behaviour and action of planning – the thoughts, desires, specifications, objectives and actions of the people who plan.

Presentation

By presentation I mean not just the final result, but also the thoughts, the logic, the creativity and communication skills that go into the preparation. Presentation implies not only presenters but also an audience or a judging panel.

Problem solving

By this I mean the skills (including patience and perseverance) required to solve something that is capable of solution, such as a puzzle, as distinct from simply trying to cope with the ordinary 'problems' (difficulties) of life.

Team building

I see this as meaning more than group cooperation. It implies the creation of some sort of structure involving the division and sharing of functions and responsibilities.

Time management

By this I mean behaviour in which individuals or groups try to organize a schedule for tasks, as distinct from people simply getting on with the job as fast as they can.

Skills/category	Creativity	Efficiency	Personal
Communication	2 3 8	9 11 12 13 14 16	17 18 19 21 22
Counselling			17
Diplomacy		9 14	19 20 21
Gender	2 8	10	18 22
Hidden agenda	6	9 14	21
Icebreaker		13	22 23
Negotiation		16	23 24
Planning	1 5 6 7 8	10 11 14 16	17 18 19 20 22
Presentation	1 3 4 6	9	19
Problem solving	4	12 13 15 16	24
Race			19 20
Team building	1 2 4 5 6 7 8	10 11 12 15	18 19 22 23
Time management	3 4	11 12 15	24

Skills/category	Creativity	Efficiency	Personal
Communication	25 27 28	34 35 36 37 40	41 43 45 46 47
Counselling		37	41 42 43 45
Diplomacy	25 30	39	44 46 47
Gender		34 36 40	48
Hidden agenda		37	41
Icebreaker	25		42 45
Negotiation	30	38 39	44
Planning	26 27 29 30 31 32	33 35 37 38 39 40	42 43 44 48
Presentation	26 28 32	40	
Problem solving	32	33 37 38 39	
Race			48
Team building	26 28 29 30 31 32	33 34 35 36 37 40	42
Time management	32	33	

Introducing the events

Objectives

One decision to make is whether to spell out the objectives in the briefing. No objectives are mentioned in the participants' Briefing sheets. This gives you the option of not revealing the objectives until the debriefing. A possible advantage of setting out the objectives when introducing the event is to avoid misunderstandings; a possible disadvantage is that the participants might modify their behaviour to fit the objectives rather than behave naturally.

In general, my advice would be to say as little as possible in the briefing and let events shape themselves.

In particular, it is vital to avoid misleading words. If you introduce a simulation as a 'game' and then afterwards complain that the participants competed rather than cooperated, or indulged in 'fun and games', then you are in a weak position if they retort, 'You should not have called it a game'. A big difference between 'games' and 'simulations' is that games finish when they end, whereas with simulations the situation can be envisaged as a continuance, as in life. After a simulation, 'winning' can be regarded as uncaring and successful 'bluffs' can be regarded as despicable frauds, much to the surprise and dismay of the gamesters.

Job allocation

In many of these events the participants have specific jobs, often different jobs. It is in keeping with the idea of equal rights that pervades this book, that these roles (jobs, functions, duties) should be allocated at random. This means, of course, that friends (or perhaps cliques) will be broken up and this may initially be resented until participants get used to the idea. If you are in a situation where a gender or racial division does exist (this can usually be ascertained by glancing at who is sitting where), then it is probably a good idea for you to bring this random allocation out into the open at the briefing, explain your reasons for it (more fair, more professional, more interesting, more democratic) and ask if anyone objects.

Try to avoid involving yourself in the randomization. It is best simply to mark the Briefing sheets (or use identity tags) and turn them face down, letting the participants pick their own.

Briefing sheets

The Briefing sheets tell the participants what they need to know about the situation. In most cases it would probably be equally effective for the facilitator not to use the Briefing sheets but to summarize the position verbally. However, the Briefing sheets:

* provide an insurance against forgetting to mention a key point and having to interrupt the action later to say 'Sorry, I should have told you that...'
* help in avoiding an overbriefing, of saying too much, of telling the participants what decisions to take, of dropping hints, guiding them and generally undermining their authority as decision makers.

In the Method section of each event, the facilitator is advised to retrieve all the Briefing sheets *before* the action begins. The reason for this is to avoid unnecessary clutter and thereby increase the degree of authenticity and plausibility of the event. There are no Briefing sheets in real life.

Authenticity

Before running any event, consider whether any reasonable and appropriate steps can be made to increase the authenticity of the occasion. This depends entirely on the working environment. Is it a boardroom or a prison, a lecture theatre or a penthouse suite?

What should always be done is to remove any personal clutter that is inappropriate – coats, briefcases, umbrellas, timetables and all non-relevant documents. Usually these objects can be placed on a side table.

Little touches can often make a big difference. An event that envisages a coffee break can be enhanced by having refreshments delivered to the room. A boardroom environment can be enhanced by pens and notepads and perhaps glasses and a carafe of water. However, avoid trying to introduce so much authenticity that it becomes a distraction.

An essential consideration is the furniture and the layout of the room. For example, all icebreakers envisage people standing up and moving around, so if an icebreaker is run in a lounge with deep armchairs, some special arrangements will be needed to ensure a flow of traffic. Some events require changes in the furniture halfway through. For example, the first stage may envisage widely separated groups, whereas the next stage could involve a team engaged in a presentation and all the other teams being a single audience. If the facilitator leaves the participants in their original groups and asks them to turn round to look at the presentation, the message received by the participants could be that the facilitator does not have a high opinion of either the event or themselves.

Some events require privacy, so it is useful to look at ways of achieving this. Groups might move out into the corridor or another room. A refreshment break in the snack bar could be used for private discussions.

The advantages of considering the question of authenticity are not limited to the plausibility of the environment. Your efforts could produce a glow of satisfaction from participants when they realize that they and the event are being treated with seriousness, consideration and imagination. This in turn can boost their feelings of autonomy and enhance their decision-making powers.

Running the events

The function of the facilitator

When running the events, the most important objective for a facilitator is invisibility. Unfortunately, the habits of instruction can make this a difficult objective to achieve. It is all too easy for a facilitator to enter the boardroom and ask the executives whether they have understood what they are supposed to do, whether they have considered drawing up an agenda, whether they realize that it is a good idea to read between the lines of the document they have just been given, etc.

The motives for trying to usurp participant autonomy are usually:

* the habit of instruction
* a genuine desire to improve the result
* a defensive measure to prevent things going wrong.

Intervention is inconsistent with the methodology. Participant autonomy is essential in these events, otherwise they become guided exercises or training sessions or tuition periods. The participants must be allowed the freedom of professionals and that includes the freedom to make mistakes. It is a good idea to reconcile oneself to the view that disasters, although not desirable, are excellent ways of learning and to remember that each event is followed by a debriefing in which lessons can be drawn from what occurred.

It follows from this that facilitators should intervene only on questions of procedure: 'Can we give a news conference?', 'Can we have another ten minutes?', 'Can we use the overhead projector?' If, however, the questions are questions of policy or substance ('Do you want us to support this proposal?' or 'Are we allowed to draw up an agenda?'), then the best reply is probably that you are not on the staff of the organization.

However, intervention is required if a participant opts out of an event and it is worthwhile for the facilitator to draw up one or two contingency plans that take into account the nature of the course and the sort of participants who are involved.

The general advice given for such situations is to start by finding out what has gone wrong. It may have nothing to do with the event itself and may be purely personal. One way of dealing with it is to use the simulated environment of the event itself, perhaps sending a message to the participant that there is a telephone call from the Managing Director, the Editor, the King or whatever role is plausible. Once the participant is withdrawn from the event it is usually fairly easy to see whether the objection is fundamental or something based on a trivial misunderstanding. If it is fundamental, then it is probably best not to argue or try to persuade the participant to continue, but to accept the decision without demur and offer alternatives. Ask whether the participant would be willing to continue in a different role or in a different group. If neither suggestion is accepted then you could suggest that the participant might like to continue as an observer or a deputy facilitator.

Trial runs

The assumption made in this book is that you have had experience of running interactive events. If you have not and if you are somewhat fearful of venturing into areas outside instructional methodology, then my advice would be for you to start with event 11, Escape. Run it with a few friends to find out what it feels like to hand over authority for decision making to the participants.

Even if you are an experienced facilitator, it is still good advice to get the real feel of an event before walking in front of the participants and running it. A full-scale test is the most reliable – using friendly volunteers who are representative of the intended participants. A second-best option is to have a shortened run through, with people actually participating, but for only part of the event (for example the beginning of a meeting). If no volunteers are available and you can find no one to advise you, the fallback position is for you to enter the event imaginatively by taking roles and changing hats and saying aloud (or at least thinking) the actual words that you would use in that role in that situation.

Time and numbers

To ask the question 'How long will the event last?' is rather like asking 'How long will the meal last?' One can give only a rough generalization unless one knows the circumstances – the type of course, the type of participants, the facilitator's attitude to debriefing and so on. So the times given in the introductions to the events should be regarded as approximations. The best way to obtain more concrete evidence is to do a trial run.

The same dependence on circumstances applies to the number of participants. The procedures are flexible. Two participants could share one role or one participant could take on two roles, for example, Also, with large numbers, the same event could be run in parallel groups simultaneously.

Running the debriefing

It is not uncommon for facilitators to feel less confident about handling the debriefing of a simulation, exercise or game than they are about running the event. Perhaps because of a lack of confidence, facilitators sometimes allow an event to overrun and the debriefing is either shortened or even omitted. In general, debriefings tend to be unimaginative. It is commonly assumed that a debriefing must consist of the facilitator asking questions and drawing conclusions. Occasionally it can take the form of a lecture in which the facilitator tells the participants what they have learned. As this book is about imaginative events it is appropriate to try to make the debriefing imaginative as well. The method of debriefing can be looked at from three aspects: assessment, style and content.

Assessment

It is worth noting that assessment is inevitable, even if there is no debriefing. Participants and facilitators cannot avoid thinking about what happened in the events and they naturally evaluate what occurred according to their normal values – educational, social and ethical. By far the greatest part of such assessments are unnoticed, occurring in private chats in the coffee bar or staff room or just meditated upon privately. Such reflections and assessments can occur and recur days, weeks, or even years after the events themselves.

If the course is designed to assess skills, this can be done formally with a structured list, as indicated in the Self-assessment sheets in events 1, 4, 7, 11, 12, 27, 32, 37, 38, and 39. These are check-lists to assess the behaviour and skills as related to the objectives. The check-lists can, of course, be used for the facilitator's own formal assessment of the participants – as individuals, or as groups or as both. These specific events are particularly amenable to formal assessments. If you wish to extend the formal assessment to the other events, then you can use the same format by listing the particular objectives for that event and have the four measures poor, fair, good and excellent. Alternatively, the assessments can be informal – covering the same points but not officially marking the results.

Style

The question of style depends on the facilitator's own attitudes: whether it is preferable to be in charge or to hand over at least some of the responsibility to the participants, whether to run a routine and safe debriefing or whether to be innovative. Here is a list of a few of the possibilities, so that you can sort out which options you favour most, which ideas you are familiar with and which procedures you are willing to try – at least as a one-off experiment.

Some options

* Allowing a committee of participants to run the debriefing, having warned them about this in advance of the event.
* Using small group debriefings, at least as a starting point.
* Using the format of a public opinion poll, with each participant being given a clip board on which they write their own question(s) and have to obtain as many answers as possible by individually interviewing other people.

* Giving responsibility to sub-committees to investigate the behaviour that occurred – the private thoughts as well as the public utterances, the rejected ideas as well as those made public.
* Deferring the debriefing for an hour or day or week in order to allow more considered (and perhaps less emotional) views to emerge.
* Negotiating with the participants the form of the debriefing in advance of the event itself.

Content

The content of the debriefing should be considered in advance because the content is likely to influence what you look for during the event itself.

The structured approach

One possibility is to have a structured approach, using a preconceived check-list of objectives and concentrate upon that.

The advantage of a structured approach is that it links the results with the objectives. The participants can see for themselves how they have got on. The relevance becomes self-evident. The participants can satisfy themselves about the reasons for participating in the event within the context of the objectives of the course. From this it is only a short step to discovering what they have gained from the experience.

The disadvantage of a structured approach is that it tends to ignore or overlook some of the most interesting and relevant events that occurred but were not predicted. Such unusual or innovative episodes, including disasters, are often the most memorable features; they are the building blocks for learning from experience, as they stimulate the imagination. In general, the 'not-so-simple' events provide the most scope for initiatives as they confer a greater degree of autonomy and choice – although this is not to say that the specific events chosen are lacking in opportunities for innovation and new ideas.

Preconceived questions

If you are running an event for the first time, you could concentrate on those questions that are mentioned in the sections on debriefing the particular events. These ideas are based on previous experiences of running the events in a variety of situations. For example, starting points are particularly well worth observing. Do the participants immediately pick up their pens as if they were diligent hermits or do they talk, discuss and examine options? Do they try to manage time or do they adopt an immediate hands-on approach and later complain that you did not give them enough time to complete the task? How do they deal with difficulties and disagreements? Such preconceived questions, however, are no substitute for your own experiences of running the same event on a previous occasion. The more familiar you are with an event, the easier you will find the task of observing, assessing and debriefing.

If you are completely new to the methodology, try to include a short debriefing session in a trial run, preferably using one of the Five simple events. When doing so, try to relax and treat it as a learning experience.

In defence of the imaginative

In my experience, some facilitators, while personally liking imaginative events, are reluctant to use them because they believe that their students (or their colleagues) will view the events as scoring high for fun, but low for relevance. For example, if one mentions that an event deals with space travellers or that the event has people applying for the job of sorcerer's apprentice, then there is a possibility that the listener will smile condescendingly. In some cases the accusation of too much fun and too little relevance is justified – when the participants behave as if they were engaged in 'fun and games'. However, even if the event *is* treated seriously and professionally, the participants and facilitator may feel somewhat guilty if they cannot immediately put their finger on the 'relevance'.

Part of the difficulty is caused by confusing 'relevance' with 'reality'. Perhaps the clearest example I can give is that judges tend to approve of extreme, hypothetical cases as such examples are often the best for illuminating basic principles of law. Although obviously lacking in *reality*, such hypotheticals can be highly *relevant*.

Another misconception is to confuse relevance with factual knowledge. Factual knowledge is relevant, but so too are skills, ethics, art, motivation and human feelings.

Although each imaginative event should be assessed on its own merits and within the context in which it is used, the following general points may be useful in arguing the case for imagination and for explaining, perhaps in the debriefing, the true relevance. Imaginative events, because they have escaped from the constraints of habit, can:

1 allow people to bypass stereotyped thinking
2 promote equality of opportunity, as distinct from a hierarchy of experts or domination by gender or race
3 encourage openness because personal (real) status is not at stake
4 enable principles to be examined without the clutter of cultural preconceptions
5 help the facilitator and participants to assess human qualities, as distinct from fact-learning
6 enhance innovative thinking and the ability to cope with change.

The objective of enhancing innovation is not so much to produce bright ideas for managerial efficiency as to widen horizons. The aim is to encourage openmindedness and to invite (or provoke) a conscious avoidance of stereotyped thinking and behaviour. In creating these events I have tried to make it easy for participants to experiment, to take different viewpoints and, on occasions, to have enough courage to challenge conventional wisdom.

Creativity areas

1 *Banana peel*

Description   In this simulation the participants are asked to invent a banana peeler and advertise it. It can be either a fun product or it can actually work.

Objectives   To enhance the skills of planning, presentation and team building.

Time and numbers   With a small number of participants, the time required is about an hour. With ten participants or more, it could take an hour and a half. The minimum number is probably five. There is no maximum.

Resources
* Briefing sheet – one copy for each participant.
* Memo from Household Techno-Products – one copy for each participant (or group).
* Ideas sheet – one copy for each participant.
* Scrap paper is essential.
* Other materials – large sheets of paper, coloured pens or markers, rulers, clips, perhaps an overhead projector – could be made available.
* Self-assessment sheet – one copy for each participant (see suggestions in **Debriefing** section).

Method   1 Divide the participants at random into groups, perhaps by marking the Briefing sheets, placing them face down and letting the participants pick their own. With five participants there could be two Designer groups of two, plus one Coordinator. With ten participants there could be four Designer groups of two, with two Coordinators. With 20 participants there could be 6 Designer groups of 3 (or 3 groups of 6) and 2 Coordinators.

2 Hand out the Ideas sheets – one to each participant – plus one copy of the Memo to each participant (or one copy to each group). Allocate the pens, paper, etc., to the groups or have a resources table. Discuss the facilities and the location for the presentations.

3 Retrieve all the Briefing sheets and discuss the timing of the simulation.

Debriefing   This is one of the Five simple events listed in the Introduction and the easiest way to debrief a simple event is to ask the participants to fill in the Self-assessment sheets individually and use the results as a basis for discussion. The alternative is to take a more flexible approach and tailor the debriefing according to the particular course, the type of participants and significant episodes that occurred during the action. The following questions and suggestions could be used as a guide not only for the debriefing but also as a check-list of the sorts of things you could watch for in the action itself. (See also **Running the debriefing**, Introduction.)

As the presentations will have explored the viability of the products, little time need be given to continuing a debate about their merits. Perhaps the teams could take it in turns to explain what difficulties they encountered in design, presentation or coordination and how they tackled them.

Was the planning cooperative? Did the Designers pick up their pens immediately and start working independently? Did they work as a team and discuss options? Did they make any plans about who should do what? The Briefing sheet and Memo stressed the desirability of cooperation within teams and between teams. How much communication was there between teams? Did some teams compete? Were participants aware that the Managing Director might not be overjoyed to discover that some staff had turned a cooperative feasibility study into a competitive event?

Did teams concentrate so much on design that they forgot about the advertising? Were the presentations planned well in advance or left to the last minute? Did only one member of each team make the presentation?

Did the Coordinators *work* together or just *sit* together? Did they go round the groups regularly? Did they discuss whether to go as individuals or as a team? Did they discuss their procedures and aims at an early stage or just hope for the best? How early did they discuss the timing and order of the presentations or was this hastily improvized at the last minute?

In this simulation you are Designers employed by Household Techno-Products and your boss has asked you to invent a banana peeler and plan to advertise it. The procedure is outlined in the Memo from the Managing Director.

Communication between teams is encouraged in feasibility studies at Household Techno-Products and with each study a different team of Designers takes on the job of coordination. Their function is to facilitate communication, to encourage diversity and to avoid duplication of effort. They decide on the order and timing of the presentations and arrange that other teams are seated in a good position to observe and allow questions after each presentation.

The presentations are regarded as hypotheses, not competitions. They can be experimental to explore various ways of advertising and demonstrating the products so that Designers can learn from each other. The Coordinators sum up after the presentations. They do not announce 'winners'.

Household Techno-Products

MEMO

From: MD
To: Designers

Following the success of some of our 'gimmicky' lines, I want you to test the feasibility of designing and advertising a banana peeler. I know of no such device, so if you are successful we could be first in the field and could use this as part of our image-building publicity.

The device itself can be either a practical gadget that does work or it can be a joke device that does not work. It could be marketed expensively for 'the person who has everything' or marketed as a cheap toy.

Operate in the usual way - Designer teams and Coordinators - and have presentations plus comments and discussion. Communicate not only within teams but between teams.

If a team is unable to think of any design for a banana peeler it should devise advertisements. Remember that in the planning stage a poor idea is much better than no idea at all. All ideas, good and bad, have contributed to our development as an expanding enterprise in the forefront of the market.

Good luck with this one.

Group	Design idea	Presentation idea	Comments

Self-assessment sheet   1   Banana peel

How did you begin?   For example, did you start by picking up your pens and working independently? Did you have a brainstorming session? Did you start by discussing options?

Did you allocate different jobs? For example, did you make someone the boss? Did you put someone in charge of designing or advertising or presentation?

Looking back, did you give too much attention to one aspect? For example, did you concentrate on design and neglect presentation? Did you concentrate on your own team and neglect cooperation with other teams?

How did you handle disagreements?

How do you assess yourself?

Skills	Poor	Fair	Good	Excellent
Creativity				
Planning				
Presentation				
Team building				
(Other)				

How do you assess your team?

Skills	Poor	Fair	Good	Excellent
Creativity				
Planning				
Presentation				
Team building				
(Other)				

2 *Executess*

Description This is a simulation in which editorial staff of the new international women's business magazine *Executess* are asked to draw up a consistent house style that identifies gender.

Objectives To enhance the skills of communication and team building in a simulation involving gender.

Time and numbers Allow about one hour if there is one team and more than an hour if there are two or more teams. The minimum number is probably four. There is no maximum.

Resources
* Briefing sheet – one copy for each participant.
* Memo from Lord Delta – one copy for each participant.
* Suggestions sheet – one copy for each participant.
* Scrap paper.

Method
1 Hand out one copy of the Briefing sheet to each participant. If there are 15 or more participants, run the simulation as 2 separate but parallel events and allocate room space for the 2 events.

2 Hand out the Memo and Suggestions sheet, one to each participant. However, in keeping with the suggestions in Lord Delta's Memo, do not subdivide the groups within the same event and preferably do not mention any of the options set out by Lord Delta. If you are asked questions such as 'Do you want us to organize ourselves into pairs?' this indicates that they are not familiar with the methodology. You could reply 'I am not on the staff of *Executess*'.

3 Make scrap paper available. Retrieve the copies of the Briefing sheet. Set whatever deadline might be required.

Debriefing As Lord Delta's aim of proliferating gender words is the reverse of accepted wisdom, it is likely that this will be an early topic in the debriefing. How viable is *Executess*?

During the event, did any participants find that their personal beliefs were interfering with their professional approach? Did emotions impair efficiency? Did they waste time arguing about Lord Delta's policy rather than on implementing it?

Was any time spent in deciding whether to work individually or in small groups or as a full committee? If so, who made the decision and how? Did the arrangement (or lack of arrangement) fulfil Lord Delta's request for 'lots of suggestions'.

If most participants worked in teams, how much communication was there within teams and between teams? To what extent was there team building? Did anyone get the job of organizer? Was there a lot of duplicated effort? Did anyone keep track of what was going on or keep an eye on the time? If there was more than one group, did anyone suggest that it might be a good idea to allocate the last ten minutes to a comparison of lists?

How inventive (humorous, pertinent, evocative) were their ideas? Did they consider only those words with masculine connotations and ignore words like nurse, sister (in charge of nurses), nanny, midwife, housewife? If some participants were unable to think of new words, did they lapse into immobility or busy themselves by doing what they could to help the organization, even if it was only getting the coffee (which, incidentally, is a service not be despised and can win friends).

This is a simulation in which editorial staff of the new international women's business magazine *Executess* are asked to draw up a consistent house style that identifies gender.

You will receive a Memo from your boss, Lord Delta, plus a Suggestions sheet.

The background information is that *Executess* is owned by Lord Delta, a publishing magnate and formerly sportsman, playboy and customs officer. As customs officer he discovered that it was inefficient to have the job more or less exclusively reserved as a male occupation as women customs officers often had more patience, were less intimidating and were quicker to spot deceptions.

Lord Delta is a good employer who pays excellent salaries. Although not a tyrant he usually gets his own way. Your own position is that of any other professional journalist. You do not have to agree with the views of your employer, but you are expected to do the work for which you are being paid

MEMO

From: Delta
To: Editorial staff

Congratulations on an excellent first issue. It sold out. Although we expect a small drop of sales for the second edition, I am quite certain we will establish ourselves as a leading magazine.

Of the issue itself, I was particularly impressed, stimulated and amused by 'A man's place is in the home'. In fact, all items seemed to me to be well-written, thought-provoking and on the side of human beings.

However, we are lacking a consistent house style for gender. As you know, I think women are too important to be deprived of their identity by having their gender words deleted from the dictionary. Executess is a new gender word for the dictionary. Women need gender words. They need identity, not nonentity.

I want you to draw up some guidance for my consideration about words we can adopt that show whether the person we are speaking about is a man or woman – such as empress and emperor, witch and warlock, bride and groom, lady and lord, queen and king. Do not restrict yourself to adding 'ess' on to everything, I am not afraid of using invented words.

You could work as individuals and go round soliciting comments on your ideas using the Suggestions sheet or you could work in pairs or operate as a committee. Whatever you do, I want it to be effective. I don't want a tiny list of three or four words you can all agree on, I want lots of suggestions.

Suggestions sheet

Executess

Words	Suggested by	Comments

3 *Historical words*

Description This is a simulation about presentations to rehabilitate 'core' words.

Objectives To enhance the skills of communication, presentation and time management.

Time and numbers Allow an hour or two, depending on numbers. The more people the more time is taken up by the presentations. The minimum number is five – two pairs and a committee member. With 20 or more participants, you could divide the simulation into 2 parallel and simultaneous events.

Resources
* Briefing sheet – one copy for each participant.
* Doctrinal entry form – one for each pair.
* Scrap paper and perhaps display equipment – charts, overhead projector, etc.

Method

1 If the participants are unfamiliar with simulations, point out that the methodology requires professionalism, not playacting.

2 Hand out the Briefing sheets. Discuss the facilities that are available, including the geographical location of chairs, tables and the presentation area. This area may have to be set up by rearranging the tables after the groups have finished the preparations for their presentations. Choose at random the Committee and randomly divide the rest of the participants into pairs.

3 Give each pair one copy of the Doctrinal entry form and give a copy to the Committee for information.

4 Make scrap paper available. Retrieve all the Briefing sheets.

5 Set a time limit for the start of the debriefing, but do not set time limits within the event itself. The Committee is responsible for the timing of the presentations. If, as the event proceeds, you conclude that the timing arrangements are so inefficient that the participants will not get in all the presentations before the deadline, sit on your hands and think of the debriefing.

Debriefing Assuming that the Committee organized an effective schedule and prevented any loquacious members from overrunning their time, the debriefing could start with you congratulating all the participants and asking each group to reveal what words they considered but did not use. A waste paper basket is often a revealing source of material showing the development of creativity.

One key issue is whether they communicated well. For example, was each pair a team or was it simply two individuals sitting next to each other? Did they start by picking up their pens or did they talk about procedures?

Did they spend so much time discussing words and definitions that they neglected to make an adequate plan for the presentation? Did they divide up different aspects of the presentation, perhaps having one person dealing with history and another with current usage?

In making their presentations did they behave as if they were speaking to students or to learned members of a serious, albeit somewhat eccentric, society? Did their speeches embrace any courtesies – 'learned members', 'distinguished lexicographers', 'honourable historians'? Did they imagine themselves into the event by saying, 'As is customary on such occasions, I will...', or 'As I mentioned at our last gathering...'?

Was there any drift into the wrong methodology? Did the presenters behave as historians or as clowns? Were members of the audience professional and respectful or did they behave as if they were in a party game?

This is a simulation about presentations to rehabilitate 'core' words.

You are all members of the Historical Words Society and attend a session in which pairs of members make presentations about rehabilitating 'core' words. The Committee of the HWS is responsible for the timing and order of the presentations and making sure that there is sufficient time for questions after each presentation.

The background is that these meetings occur every month or two. Although some outsiders regard the Society as eccentric, there is no question about its seriousness. However, as far as you are concerned, you are not required to be erudite in *fact*, only erudite in *fiction*. Your job is to invent plausible meanings or submeanings or derivations or historical antecedents of well-known words.

For example, you might explain that 'confer' originally related to mediaeval princes manipulating their subjects under the guise of consultation. This, you could explain, is the origin of modern slang where 'to con' means 'to trick'. Similarly the root of 'fer' meant pass or passage, as in 'refer', which means repeated passage, to pass again, as in the phrase 'refer it back'. So the origin of the word 'confer' meant to pass or implement a policy by deception, by tricking people into the belief that they were being consulted.

The more weird your invention the more plausibly you should seek to present it, delving into its history and giving examples that could be entirely fictitious. Avoid jokes, espouse earnestness.

If any team cannot think of a suitable core word, they must approach another team who are honour bound to supply them with one or more of their spare core words. It is the custom of the Society that both members of a team should speak during a presentation.

Historical Words Society

Doctrinal entry form

Please write down the word or words that you wish to examine in your presentation, so that these can be announced by the Committee at the beginning of your presentation and also repeated at the end, after the questions and answers, as a formal tribute to your efforts. A brief comment against each word would also be appreciated.

Words	Comments

4 *Marbledown*

Description
A simulation in which teams have to build a device made of paper and paper-clips that brings a marble down from a height to a located position and participants present and demonstrate their device.

Objectives
To enhance the skills of presentation, problem solving, team building and time management.

Time and numbers
The minimum number is probably five (one participant taking all three Tutor roles, and two teams of two Designers). In this case the event could last about an hour. With more teams, which means more time for presentations, about one and a half to two hours should be allowed. There is no maximum because with large numbers the simulation could be run as two (or more) parallel events.

Resources
* Briefing sheet – one copy for each participant.
* Construction specifications sheet – one for each design team.
* Construction materials for each design team:

  * 10 sheets of paper
  * 20 paper-clips
  * one pair of scissors
  * a 1-foot (or 30-cm) ruler.

* Three Comments sheets – one for each tutor.
* Scrap paper and perhaps display equipment – coloured pens, charts, overhead projector, etc.
* Self-assessment sheet – one copy for each participant (see suggestions in **Debriefing** section).

Method
1 Before the event begins prepare the 'packages' of construction materials and work out (at least roughly) the size and number of groups. With nine participants there could be three Tutors and either three teams of two or two teams of three Designers. With 20 participants there could be 4 Design teams of 4, 3 Tutors and 1 Helper (or Reporter).

2 Allocate jobs at random, perhaps by marking the Briefing sheets, placing them face down and asking the participants to pick their own sheets.

3 Discuss the facilities that are available, including any presentation equipment. The geographical location of chairs, tables and the presentation area(s) could be very important because of the need to have as level a surface as possible. If the presentation area is different from the construction area(s), consider in advance the question of transport. It would be unfair if the participants had to construct their devices without realizing the need to move them to a demonstration area. There could be a special area for the Tutors to meet in private to discuss their procedures, which could be one side of the room or a corridor or a separate room.

4 Hand out the Construction specifications sheet – one copy to each Design team, and give a copy to the Tutors for information. Allocate at random the Comments sheets to the Tutors.

5 Retrieve all the Briefing sheets. Fix a deadline for the end of the event. Hand out the construction materials to the Design teams.

Debriefing

This is one of the Five simple events listed in the Introduction and the easiest way to debrief a simple event is to ask the participants to fill in the Self-assessment sheets individually and use the results as a basis for discussion. The alternative is to take a more flexible approach and tailor the debriefing according to the particular course, the type of participants and significant episodes that occurred during the action. The following questions and suggestions could be used as a guide not only for the debriefing but also as a check-list of the sorts of things you could watch for in the action itself. (See also **Running the debriefing**, Introduction.)

As everyone will have seen the demonstrations and presentations, little time need be spent on discussing the merits of each construction, unless, of course, the participants are engaged in design or construction in real life.

A starting point could be a factual explanation by each team of what was *not* observed by everyone – the abandoned first thoughts, the process of decision making – and how the participants perceived and tackled the assignment. This explanation should include contributions from the tutors about how they tackled their problems of observing, organizing and judging.

How effective was the team building and time management? Did teams concentrate so much on design and construction that they neglected to plan the presentation? If they complain afterwards that they did not have enough time (a usual complaint) had they made any attempt to divide up what time they had? Were the presentations team efforts done with style and authority or did they amount to little more than placing the marble at the top of the device?

How effective were the Tutors in their summing up? Were they authoritative and friendly? Had they made any perceptive observations on their Comments sheets? Did they take on board their own specialities? Did they say 'As a psychologist I was particularly impressed by the way you handled stress' or 'As a business consultant I would like to congratulate you on your team building and time management'?

This is a simulation set in an Engineering College in which teams have to build a device make of paper and paper-clips that brings a marble down from a height to a located position and then present and demonstrate their device.

You are either third-year engineering Students or you are Tutors (the class tutor, who is an engineer, a psychologist from the Psychology Department and a business consultant who often comes to the College for the purpose of advising students).

You will all receive the Construction specifications sheet, and each Tutor will have a Comments sheet relating to the particular speciality.

What is not explained, but what you all know, is that you are at a prestigious engineering college and the Engineering Degree examination involves a group construction test. This occasion is the final practise test that takes place a few weeks before the examination itself.

Everyone, including the Tutors, were involved in the test at the end of the first year, which involved nails and soap, and the second-year test, when the main materials were three elastic bands and two rulers. Last year the class Tutor congratulated the Students on their all-round improvement, the psychology Tutor advised them to concentrate on communicating their ideas and working together, while the third Tutor, the business consultant, said that there seemed to have been only a slight improvement in their presentations.

The Tutors are responsible for the timing of the presentations, which must start on time even if the devices are not complete. The schedule must include time for other teams to ask questions after each presentation. The Tutors must also allow time for their own comments, which could include comparisons with what happened in previous years.

Construction specifications sheet

Project Marbledown

For **Project Marbledown** you will be provided with the following materials for construction purposes: 10 sheets of paper, 20 paper-clips, a pair of scissors, a 1-foot (or 30-cm) ruler and 1 marble.

A device must be constructed for the marble to pass (roll or drop) from a ruler's length above the construction surface. It must not be touched by hand after the point of release, which must be done by placing (not impelling) the marble at some point on the device. The area for the device must be no wider at base than 12 inches (30 cm) at any point. It must be free-standing and not be secured to the surface by paper-clips or in any other way. The marble must come to rest in an area six inches by six inches (15 cm by 15 cm) which must be outside the base area. The surface of this resting area must be free of material and the boundary should be marked in some way. The marble should not hit the boundary. (If the surface itself is uneven, this will be taken into account by the Tutors.)

In making your device, you are permitted to bend (or break) the paper-clips. If you wish to do so, you can incorporate the scissors, the ruler or both into the construction itself.

You will have scrap paper, but this must not be used for construction purposes. Three demonstration runs are permitted as part of a presentation of the device.

The Tutors will comment on:

1 the effectiveness of the device
2 its elegance and imaginative features
3 the presentation (high marks can be awarded even if the device fails)
4 communication skills, team building and time management.

Comments sheet: class tutor

Type of construction considered but rejected.

_____

_____

_____

_____

_____

_____

Engineering difficulties encountered.

_____

_____

_____

_____

_____

_____

General comments.

_____

_____

_____

_____

_____

_____

Comments sheet: psychology tutor

Did the team think as a team or did individuals grab the materials?

_____

_____

_____

_____

_____

Did they learn from their mistakes?

_____

_____

_____

_____

_____

How did they cope with stress in the final minutes before the deadline?

_____

_____

_____

_____

General comments.

_____

_____

_____

_____

_____

Comments sheet: business consultant

Did the Students use scrap paper to outline their ideas?

_____

_____

_____

Was there any team building and time management?

_____

_____

_____

_____

_____

How effective were communication skills and decision-making skills?

_____

_____

_____

_____

_____

_____

_____

General comments.

_____

_____

_____

_____

_____

_____

How did you begin? For example, did you start by working independently? Did you have a brainstorming session? Did you start by discussing options? Did you discuss the time factor?

Did you allocate different jobs? For example, did you make someone the boss? Did you put someone in charge of keeping an eye on the time?

Looking back, did you give too much attention to one aspect? For example, did the Students concentrate on design and neglect presentation, or concentrate on their own ideas and neglect other people's ideas? Did the Tutors concentrate on observing and neglect the task of devising clear procedures for the presentations?

How did you handle disagreements?

How effective were the presentations by the Students and the assessments of the Tutors? Did the Students simply place the marble on the device and fail to mention what had happened in the design process? Did the Tutors give a good summing up? Did any Tutor mention their own speciality – 'Speaking as a business consultant I liked the way you worked as a team'?

How do you assess yourself?

Skills	Poor	Fair	Good	Excellent
Creativity				
Presentation				
Problem solving				
Team building				
Time management				
(Other)				

How do you assess your team?

Skills	Poor	Fair	Good	Excellent
Creativity				
Presentation				
Problem solving				
Team building				
Time management				
(Other)				

5 *Singing refrigerator*

Description   This is a simulation about Managers in four Departments of a white goods manufacturing company who have been asked to draw up a five-question Questionnaire about the marketing potential of a singing refrigerator.

Objectives   The objectives are to enhance the skills of planning and team building.

Time and numbers   It is suitable for any number above three. There are four Departmental tags. With six participants there could be one group of six with a sharing of jobs or two groups of three, in which case two jobs will be taken by one participant. With one group, the event should last between half an hour and an hour. With more than one group, the event will probably last more than an hour because of the extra time needed in the debriefing to describe, compare and comment on the Questionnaires.

Resources
* Briefing sheet – one for each participant.
* Memo from Managing Director – one for each participant.
* Blank Questionnaire – one for each group, with spares available.
* Departmental tags – a set of four for each group.
* Scrap paper.

Method   1 Hand out the Briefing sheets – one copy for each participant – perhaps marking the sheets in order to allocate the participants at random into groups of four.

2 Hand out to each group the Managing Director's Memo – one copy for each participant. Randomly hand out the Departmental tags. Give one copy of the blank questionnaire to each group and make spare copies available.

3 Make sure each team has an adequate supply of scrap paper. Retrieve the Briefing sheets. Set a deadline for the event.

Debriefing   If there were several groups, the first few minutes can be taken up with reporting not only the questions used but also those that were considered but rejected.

As the merits (and perhaps the demerits) of a singing refrigerator were explored during the event, the debriefing will probably concentrate on the objectives of planning and team building, plus the imagination shown during the event.

As there were four Departments, but five questions, it was not possible simply to allocate one question to each Department. So what happened? Did they plan any procedure or just get on with the job as they saw fit? Did they start with a brainstorming session and, if so, was this planned and intended or did it arise by accident? Did each Manager work independently? What happened if disputes arose in the team? Were there any voting or any veto arrangements? Did their planning include identifying the potential market and, if so, did this include the export market?

Did they build a team and envisage what would happen when the results of the Questionnaire became known? Did they put the Company's interests first or the interests of their own Departments? Did anything unexpected occur, such as the formation of two sub-committees – advertising/design and finance/sales?

This is a simulation about Managers of different Departments of a white goods manufacturing company who have to draw up a five-question Questionnaire about the marketing potential of a singing refrigerator.

You have the job of a Manager in Kitchen Innovations Inc. The Departments you represent are Advertising, Design, Finance and Sales. The procedure is set out in a Memo from the Managing Director. What the Memo does not tell you, but what you know already is that, despite the polite and accommodating words, the Managing Director can be a tyrant and has never shown any hesitation in firing people who fail to meet her standards for planning and team building.

Kitchen Innovations Inc.

Memo

From: MD
To: Managers of Advertising, Design, Finance and Sales Departments

As you know, it is now possible for us to build a singing refrigerator. I want to use an independent market research organization. This organization charges according to the number of questions asked. I have decided that there must be five questions.

I hope you will be able to reach agreement on five questions that cover most or all the important questions of interest to your individual Departments.

If you find yourself in a situation in which you cannot agree on five questions, I would be obliged if you would submit individual lists of your choices and I would personally choose five questions from the lists. Please do the best you can to work together.

Questionnaire for a singing refrigerator

Name:

Department:

_____

Question one:

_____

Question two:

_____

Question three:

_____

Question four:

_____

Question five:

_____

Any comments:

------------ fold here ------------

Advertising

------------ fold here ------------

Design

------------ fold here ------------

Finance

------------ fold here ------------

Sales

6 *Tax image*

Description   This is a simulation in which Executives of an advertising company deal with a request from a Third-World oil-producing country for a campaign to make the paying of taxes less unpopular.

Objectives   To enhance the skills of planning, presentation and team building.

Time and numbers   Allow about one hour for one team, an hour and a half for more than one. The minimum is two or three participants and there is no maximum as the simulation could be run as two parallel events. With more than one team, the debriefing will take longer because of opportunities for explanations, comparisons and comments.

Resources
* Briefing sheet – one copy for each participant.
* Memo from Managing Director – one copy for each participant.
* Recommendations and comments form – one copy for each group, with spares available.
* Scrap paper.

Method   1 Hand out the Briefing sheets – one copy to each participant.

2 Do not discuss any procedures for randomizing groups as the Managing Director's Memo says this is the responsibility of the staff. For the same reason do not discuss the organization of the presentations. If, during the event, it becomes clear that there is no effective organization, take a deep breath and do nothing.

3 Hand out the Memos – one to each participant. Make available copies of the Recommendations and comments form, scrap paper and any facilities that are available for the presentations.

4 Retrieve the Briefing sheets.

Debriefing   The Managing Director requested the staff to divide at random into groups. Did they do this or simply sit down with their friends? Did anyone suggest any method for random grouping? Was anyone appointed to organize the presentations? Did they discuss organization in an organized way or simply concentrate on the tax campaign and hope for the best?

As well as drawing up a campaign for making tax paying less unpopular, did they consider who would need to be consulted or informed about its implementation? Did they assume that all such matters would be decided by the client?

Did they consider questions of costs? Did they consider whether or not their ideas had legal and/or moral implications?

In making their presentations, how helpful were the other groups in making suggestions, asking for clarifications or giving advice? Were some groups over-critical of others in the hope that their own ideas would 'win' or were they behaving cooperatively as part of an agency?

Did they discuss how the project should be given to the client – in writing or perhaps a personal presentation at the Finance Ministry of the Third World country? Such a decision would help determine the suitability of the presentation. If their recommendation was that the project should be presented in writing, they could write at least an outline, whereas if they envisaged a personal presentation they had the option of presenting it to their colleagues as if their colleagues were the client.

You are Executives in Apex Advertising and Financial Agency, which has been asked by the government of a Third-World oil-producing country to devise a campaign to make the paying of taxes less unpopular. (If you feel that your inventive skills are hampered by the vagueness of the term 'Third World', you can select a geographical region, but do not pick a real country.)

You will receive a Memo from your Managing Director explaining the procedure, plus copies of the Agency's Recommendation and comments form.

What you are not told, because you know it already, is that the Managing Director is less than pleased with the behaviour of staff during the past year. A number of potentially valuable clients have been lost through poor team work and poor communication.

Memo

From: Managing Director
To: Advertising staff

We have been asked by a Third-World oil-producing country to devise a campaign to make the paying of tax more popular or, to put it more accurately, less unpopular.

The client has proposed that we pay for the campaign initially. We would be refunded by a priority allocation from the monies received in extra tax revenue. Once the whole cost has been paid, the client's suggestion is that we would be paid five per cent of the extra tax revenue over a subsequent period of five years.

I want you to divide into random groups of between two and four and come up with ideas for the campaign. If you are unhappy with the financial proposals, outline your preferred alternative.

I want each group in turn to present their ideas to the other groups and allow time for questions and suggestions. At the end of the presentations I hope you can all agree on a package of ideas that I can put before the Board of Directors. Needless to say, the matter is of considerable importance and may affect your own futures. If we can obtain the contract for this campaign we can use it to enhance our image at home and overseas.

Recommendations and comments form

Case: Third World Tax Raising

Name:

Group	Proposal	Comments

7 *The Trap*

Description A restaurant chain – Theme Dining Company – has commissioned four Experts dealing with advertising, decor, logo and restaurant layout to produce a feasibility study for a restaurant to be called The Trap.

Objectives To enhance the skills of planning and team building.

Time and numbers The event should take about an hour. There are four Experts in each team, so the minimum number is four. There is no maximum, as separate events can be run in parallel. With more teams, which means more presentations, allow an hour and a half.

Resources
* Briefing sheet – one copy for each participant.
* Memo from the Theme Dining Company – one copy for each participant.
* Job tags – a set of four for each group.
* Layout sheet – one copy for each group (with spares if needed).
* Scrap paper.
* Self-assessment sheet – one copy for each participant (see suggestions in **Debriefing** section).

Method

1 Hand out the Briefing sheets – one to each participant – perhaps marking the sheets to help the random selection of teams of four. If the numbers do not divide equally by four, you could give one or two people the function of Assistant to the experts.

2 Hand out the Memos – one copy to each participant.

3 Seat the participants at their tables and hand out the Job tags, face down, letting the participants pick their own. Give the layout Expert one or two copies of the Layout sheets.

4 Make scrap paper available. Retrieve the Briefing sheets.

5 Set a time limit for the start of the debriefing.

Debriefing This is one of the Five simple events listed in the Introduction and the easiest way to debrief a simple event is to ask the participants to fill in the Self-assessment sheets individually and use the results as a basis for discussion. The alternative is to take a more flexible approach and tailor the debriefing according to the particular course, the type of participants and significant episodes that occurred during the action. The following questions and suggestions could be used as a guide not only for the debriefing but also as a check-list of the sorts of things you could watch for in the action itself. (See also **Running the debriefing**, Introduction.)

If there are several groups, the debriefing could start with a series of mini-debriefings in which each group debriefs itself and reports its findings to the other groups.

Team building skills in this event can be assessed by the extent to which group members worked together. If they immediately picked up their pens and worked on their own advertising, logos, decor and layouts, they behaved like diligent hermits not members of a team.

Did anyone suggest procedures – for example, starting with a brainstorming session? Did anyone take the chair, formally or informally? Did they divide into sub-committees to produce ideas – such as advertising/logo and decor/layout?

The creativity skills in this event centre on the problem of a name for the restaurant that may seem unappealing or even repulsive. This means either using 'trap' to mean anything other than entrapment or making a virtue of the seeming repulsion, as in the case of a type of chocolate pudding with the name Mississippi Mud Pie. Everyone knows that it is not real mud and that real entrapment traps are not advertised as such to their intended victims. Other types of trap include a light vehicle, a device to release a clay pigeon, a tactic in a game such as chess, a police speed trap, a tender trap, an exit as in the case of a trap door and so on. The *type* of trap should be a feature of the restaurant's layout. For example, if the trap referred to a trap door a (mock) device might be more easily installed if the restaurant was on two floors rather than one. If the trap was a mouse trap the layout might be divided into alcoves or rooms named after types of cheese.

If there is more than one team it should be easy to compare different types of creativity, although it is probably best to avoid making adverse comparisons.

You are four Experts employed by the Theme Dining Company who have been asked to produce a feasibility study for a restaurant to be called The Trap. One Expert is responsible for advertising, another for decor, a third for the logo and the fourth for the layout of the restaurant.

The Theme Dining Company owns a chain of restaurants each devoted to an individual theme, such as mountains, windows, bicycles, stations. The aim of the chain is to make eating a 'fun' occasion – fun in the sense of being interesting, amusing and perhaps provocative.

You will receive Job tags, a Memo from the Theme Dining Company and the layout Expert will be given one or two copies of the Layout sheet.

Theme Dining Company

Memo

From: Executive Director, TDC
To: Experts on advertising, decor, logo and restaurant layout

Your instructions are to work as a team to produce a feasibility study for a restaurant to be called The Trap. Your job is to produce:

(a) a draft sample of the advertising
(b) at least one draft logo
(c) a brief description of the decor, mentioning any features
(d) one (or two) sheets of layout, showing roughly the location of tables, features, etc.

The restaurant will be on a site adjacent to an out-of-town shopping complex. It will be rectangular in shape and will have two floors. There will be doors in the centre of the short sides. It would be possible to relocate the doors or have additional doors if this was essential to the theme. The staircase is marked on the plan, but you can, if you think the expense justifies it, make suggestions for moving the staircase or adding a second staircase.

The dining area can be located on one floor or on both, provided it does not occupy more than half of the total space available, as the other half will be occupied by the kitchen, offices and toilets. If the dining area was fully occupied by tables for 4, there would be room for about 30 tables. The number of tables you recommend will presumably be less than this figure to allow space for theme objects or partitions. You do not need to draw individual tables and chairs, just give an indication of the layout of the room or rooms. Please leave blank the areas for kitchen, etc., as these areas will be dealt with by another team of experts.

One key decision you should make is whether it should be an up-market restaurant or not. However, the financial side itself does not concern you.

We are looking to you for an imaginative and appealing treatment of the theme.

------------ fold here ------------

Advertising

------------ fold here ------------

Decor

------------ fold here ------------

Logo

------------ fold here ------------

Layout

How did you begin? For example, did you start by working independently? Did you have a brainstorming session? Did you start by discussing options?

Looking back, did you give too much attention to one aspect? For example, did you concentrate on designing the layout and decor and neglect the advertising and the logo? Did you push on your own ideas and neglect other people's suggestions?

Did you allocate different jobs? For example, did you make someone the boss? Did you put someone in charge of keeping an eye on the time or of coordinating the ideas?

How did you handle disagreements?

How do you assess yourself?

Skills	Poor	Fair	Good	Excellent
Creativity				
Planning				
Team building				
(Other)				

How do you assess your team?

Skills	Poor	Fair	Good	Excellent
Creativity				
Planning				
Team building				
(Other)				

8 *Weldo Junction*

Description This is a simulation about a plan by the City Council of Weldo Junction to attract visitors to the city – a city that outsiders regard as a joke.

Objectives To enhance the skills of communication, planning and team building in a situation involving the issue of gender.

Time and numbers Groups should not be larger than about six. There are no job descriptions as such, nor any presentations (you could build these in if you wish). With one group, the event should last about an hour, or possibly longer depending on the thoroughness with which they deal with their draft proposals. With more than one group, probably an hour and a half should be allowed in order to have sufficient time in the debriefing for explanations, comparisons and comments about the work of the different groups.

Resources
* Briefing sheet – one copy for each participant.
* News item from the *Weldo Junction Gazette* – one copy for each participant.
* Scrap paper and, perhaps, other facilities, such as large sheets of paper.

Method
1 If there are eight or more participants, divide them at random into groups of between four and six participants and run the simulation as parallel simultaneous events.

2 Hand out the Briefing sheets – one copy to each participant, Discuss the facilities available.

3 Give each participant a copy of the News item.

4 Make available the scrap paper and any other facilities. Retrieve all copies of the Briefing sheet. Set a deadline.

Debriefing If there was more than one group, a good way to start is by asking groups to describe their ideas – not just the one they adopted, but also the ones they rejected.

The objectives of communication, planning and team building will probably be central to the debriefing rather than a rerun of any debate on the merits of the plans. Were the groups satisfied with their team building? Did they immediately start working as individuals? Did anyone coordinate the work or, if the team was more than two or three, did it divide into sub-committees? Did anyone, formally or informally, become leader or coordinator?

Did the participants realize that 'Getting a new image' was a headline that was not borne out by the story itself? The story was that the City Council wanted to have a campaign to attract tourism, it said nothing about changing the image or of playing down the fact that the local government was by separate and equal male and female chambers.

Did the planners attempt to use the male-female local government as a way to attract visitors – for example, by encouraging professional bodies such as psychologists or sociologists or business organizations to hold their national meetings or seminars at Weldo Junction? Did anyone mention leaflets or video presentations aimed at business and academic groups?

Did they consider what to do about the implied threat of bringing in an outside agency, for example, by pointing out that the City Council's own Publicity Department could be better placed than an outside agency to implement any plan that was agreed?

You work in the Publicity Department of Weldo Junction City Council. Weldo Junction is a city that is regarded by outsiders as a joke. A resolution recently passed by the City Council requests the Publicity Department to put forward one or, perhaps, two draft plans for a campaign to attract visitors.

How you organize yourselves is up to you.

To help you understand the background, you will receive a copy of 'Getting a new image', a recent News item in the *Weldo Junction Gazette*.

Getting a new image

WELDO JUNCTION'S Male Chamber has unanimously endorsed a resolution to start a national publicity drive to attract tourism and to set aside sufficient finances for this project.

The resolution, which originated last week in the Female Chamber, was passed without dissent at yesterday's meeting of the Male Chamber. The resolution said that the job of producing plans would be given to the town's Publicity Department and these recommendations would be considered by committees of the two Chambers. Should the plans be rejected, an outside publicity agency would be brought in.

Mr Al Patel, President of the Male Chamber, said that most of the news stories picked up by the national media were gross distortions, but that denials issued by the City's Publicity Department were invariably ignored.

Mr Patel said 'Although outsiders think it ludicrous that we should have a Male and Female Chamber, our form of local government works very well in practice. As each Chamber has the power of veto, this encourages the sexes to work together. We have a more harmonious relationship than exists in most mixed sex councils'.

The President of the Female Chamber, Mrs Rita Henderson, last night welcomed the Male Chamber's decision to approve the resolution. She told the *Gazette*, 'We are known as the town people laugh at and, as a result, we have had great difficulty attracting tourists and particularly conventions, conferences and seminars. We have excellent facilities, but the recently developed Conference and Sports Centre is losing money and our hotels and shops are not getting the business they deserve'.

Efficiency areas

9 *Designing soap*

Description   A simulation about the Alpha Television Company having separate meetings with three Production companies about proposals to produce a new soap opera. This simulation has a hidden agenda.

Objectives   To enhance the skills of communication, diplomacy and presentation.

Time and numbers   The time will probably be about an hour with small numbers. The minimum number is probably eight, which allows two people to be in each team – the three Production companies and the Television company. However, it would be possible to run the event with four participants. With large numbers, the event can be run as two separate simulations and at least an hour and a half should be allocated to allow time for explanations, comparisons and comments in the debriefing.

Resources
* Briefing sheet – one copy for each participant.
* Letter from Alpha Television Company – one copy for each group, including Alpha.
* Four confidential Memos – one each for Alpha Television Company and Beta, Gamma and Delta companies.
* Four Identity cards – one for each group.
* Scrap paper.

Method   1 Depending on numbers, decide how to organize the interviews so that the Production companies do not spend too much time waiting. Perhaps the best way is for the Television company to have twice as many members as a Production team so that it can split into two (or three) and rotate the interviews. Decide who should be in charge of timing. It could be yourself or the Television Company or a participant in the role of Timekeeper or Observer.

2 Hand out the Briefing sheets – one for each participant, perhaps marking the sheets with the name of the companies, plus Alpha Television Company, and place them face down, letting participants pick their own.

3 Separate the groups as far apart as possible. Hand out to each group (including Alpha) the Letter from Alpha Television Company to the Production companies.

4 Hand out the four confidential Memos to their respective groups, plus the Identity cards,

5 Retrieve the Briefing sheets. Discuss any time limits.

Debriefing   The hidden agenda is in the confidential Memos. The groups have different and incompatible objectives. The Television company wants to know the likely contents of the soap opera, whereas the Production companies use three different ways of *not* disclosing such information.

The first step in the debriefing could be for each group to take it in turns to read out the confidential Memos.

The next step might be to take it in turns to reveal what happened within groups, this being announced without discussion from other teams.

Once the hidden facts are disclosed, the subsequent discussion could cover a variety of issues. Which of the three strategies used by the Production companies was the most effective in the event and which would be most likely to succeed in the real world? What examples from the real world could be cited?

How effective was the communication and diplomacy? Were the presentations efficiently organized? Did the Production companies draw up any contingency plan about the contents of the soap opera in case their strategy failed and they were pressed to reveal what the soap opera would be about?

Do the participants think that hidden agendas are manipulative and undesirable?

This is a simulation about the Alpha Television Company having separate meetings about a proposed soap opera(s) with three Production companies – Beta, Gamma and Delta. You are an executive in one of the four companies.

In the first stage, the Production companies draw up plans for making a presentation to the Alpha Television Company and Alpha is considering what sort of things to look for and what sort of questions to ask.

A letter from the Alpha Television Company to the Production companies gives details of the procedures and makes the point that the finances and facilities of the Production companies are not in question and that the meetings are to look at plans for the soap opera. What the letter does not say, but what you all know, is that Alpha's last soap opera, devised by Omega Productions, was about a pop singer. It was a complete flop because of poor plot, production errors and bad casting – almost everything that could go wrong went wrong.

You will each receive a company Identity card, plus an internal Memo from your boss.

Alpha Television Company
Alphatown
Alpha

To: Beta, Gamma and Delta Production companies re. proposals for new soap opera

Thank you for agreeing to come to our Head Office next Monday to make separate presentations of your proposals for a soap opera and to answer questions.

Please feel free to cover any issues you think important, but do not go into financial matters about costs and fees. This will all be covered later in the usual way. Nor need you try to convince us that you are capable of producing a soap opera – we know from your past record that you have sufficient staff and facilities to meet this basic requirement.

What we hope to hear is a fairly general outline of your plans. How would you go about the task? How would you plan it and organize it? What are your basic ideas?

We will ask you questions, but not about finance or facilities. We are unlikely to reach a final decision immediately after your presentations and there is a possibility that we might commission more than one soap opera. We look forward to seeing you.

Alpha Television Company

MEMO

From: President, Alpha Television Company
To: Interviewers, re. soap.

Although our letter to the Production companies was written in general terms, this was in the hope of leaving them free to outline whatever ideas they think are relevant. This does not mean that you have to sit like transfixed rabbits listening to a lot of wonderful claims. You know my views on high-sounding jargon. What I want to know is the nitty gritty – what the viewer is likely to see when he, or more usually she, presses the button on the TV set.

However, I hope that you will, as usual, be exceedingly polite and friendly as befits our position and I feel quite sure you will not rush into a decision and award a contract on the spot.

Beta Productions

MEMO

From: President, Beta Productions
To: Executives in charge of soap opera presentation

Your job is to state our aims and objectives. These are of paramount importance. State what we hope to achieve – our mission, our desires, our expectations – plus some indication of how we can measure whether these objectives have been achieved.

You should not, at this stage, say anything about the contents of a possible script. I have had experience of this sort of thing – once you mention the main characters or the setting or anything specific, you will always find that they spend their time criticizing that aspect and this will divert attention away from basic objectives.

Gamma Productions

MEMO

From: President, Gamma Productions
To: Executives in charge of soap opera presentation

Your job is to identify the market – the attitudes, beliefs and interests of the potential viewers. You should state our general intention to see that the soap opera takes account of the interests of viewers.

You should not, at this stage, say anything about the contents of a possible script. I have had experience of this sort of thing – once you mention the main characters or the setting or anything specific, you will always find that they spend their time criticizing that aspect and this will divert attention away from the needs of the viewers.

Delta Productions

MEMO

From: President, Delta Productions
To: Executives in charge of soap opera presentation

Your job is to explain our organization. You should state clearly who will be in charge of what, who will liaise with whom and the procedure for both script writing and also dealing with any problems.

You should not, at this stage, say anything about the contents of a possible script. I have had experience of this sort of thing – once you mention the main characters or the setting or anything specific, you will always find that they spend their time criticizing that aspect and this diverts attention away from the basic point of how the programmes will be organized.

------------- fold here ------------

Alpha Television
Company

------------- fold here ------------

Beta Productions

------------- fold here ------------

Gamma Productions

------------- fold here ------------

Delta Productions

10 *Disharmony activator*

Description This is a simulation in which an inventor has offered an electronic manufacturing company a device to register disharmonies between people and give advice. The Directors of the company have to decide whether or not to accept the terms proposed by the inventor and how to market the device.

Objectives To enhance the skills of planning and team building.

Time and numbers This is suitable for any number, even two or three. With ten participants, divide them into two groups and run it as two simultaneous events. With one group allow an hour. With more groups – and hence more ideas to explain, compare and discuss during the debriefing – allow about an hour and a half.

Resources
* Briefing sheet – one copy for each participant.
* Report from Head of Technical Department – one for each participant.
* Scrap paper.

Method
1 Hand out the Briefing sheets – one copy for each participant.

2 Divide the participants at random into groups, perhaps by marking the Briefing sheets, turning them face down and letting the participants pick their own. Fix a time limit for the end of the meetings.

3 Hand out the Report from the Head of the Technical Department – one for each participant. Make scrap paper available.

4 Retrieve all the Briefing sheets.

Debriefing If there were several groups, arrange for some way in which they can share the information about not only what they decided, but also what options they considered and how they organized themselves. Possibly the best way to do this is for each group to conduct its own mini-debriefing and announce its findings to a meeting of all the participants.

How wide-ranging were the discussions about planning? For example, did the participants consider the export market? The remark in the Report about translating the messages into another language could have prodded the participants in that direction. Did they discuss the implications of the graded sensitivity regulator? Did they think of it only as a household device or did they consider its use in other fields, such as the social services, psychiatry, the police, business, education and training? Did they consider devising a better name for the device?

The discussion about team building could cover how they coped with a situation in which no one was officially in the chair and no one was specifically responsible for finance, sales, marketing and so forth. Did anyone pick up on one of these areas and suggest that it should be referred to the appropriate department for information and advice?

An inventor has offered an electronics company – Innovative Technos
Company – a device to register disharmonies between people and give advice.
You are the Directors and have to decide whether or not to accept the terms
proposed by the inventor and how to market the device.

Normally the Board operates by not having anyone in the chair, unless anyone
feels that they want to organize the meeting.

The only item on today's agenda is the Disharmony Activator and the only
document you will receive is a Report from the Head of the Technical
Department (who is not a member of the Board). What you know already is
that a week ago the Company was approached in confidence by an inventor
with a device called the Disharmony Frequency Oscillating Activator (DFOA).
The inventor offered the company an exclusive right to manufacture the
machine providing a royalty of 15 per cent of the sale price was paid, rising to
20 per cent after the first 1000 had been sold and 30 per cent after 5000 had
been sold.

REPORT from Head of Technical Department

I have had the DFOA for the past week and put it through some intensive tests. My conclusion is that it appears to fulfil all the claims made by its inventor.

The device is voice-activated and picks up electrical and atmospheric resonances, enabling it, in most cases, to distinguish between men and women. Our tests confirmed that this device worked well, but presumably would be less reliable if a male had a high voice and a female had a deep voice. It can distinguish between a scream of delight and a scream of pain and between laughter and swearing.

It has a bleeper and a numeric counter to register the level of disharmony. There is a message screen and about 100 colour-coded messages have been programed into the device. Blue is used for messages addressed to men, red for women, and green for both.

The messages include:

* in blue: 'You're showing a high level of annoyance – are you being reasonable?'
* in red: 'Your annoyance level is rising – are you annoyed with the man or with yourself?'
* in green 'Could you discuss it calmly?'

The messages can be programed and/or translated into another language, by either the manufacturer or by the purchaser.

Inside the lid (which can be opened by removing four screws) is an adjustable 'graded sensitivity regulator' ranging from 'shrill' to 'boom'. This means, for example, that if a woman bought the machine and moved the sensor to 'boom' it would increase the proportion of warnings to males and decrease the proportion to females.

The unit cost of the first 500 is likely to be that of an expensive television set. After 1000, the unit cost should drop to that of a cheap television set.

11 *Escape*

Description　The Space School on the planet Test has 'live bullet' courses for Space officers. Failure to escape from the labyrinth means death to the *whole* team, even though failure may have been due to lack of cooperation from just one of its members. This is a simulation, not a game.

Objectives　The objectives are to enhance the skills of communication, planning, team building and time management.

Time and numbers　Allow half an hour to an hour. Groups usually die early. However, early death can lead to a longer debriefing. It is suitable for three or more. With several groups allow about an hour because more time will be needed in the debriefing for explanations, comparisons and discussion.

Resources
* Briefing sheets – one copy for each participant.
* Room cards – one cut out pack of 26 for each group.
* Information cards – four for each group.
* 17-hour schedule – one for each group.
* A table (or other suitable surface) for each group, plus ample space between groups.
* Scrap paper.
* Self-assessment sheet – one copy for each participant (see suggestions in **Debriefing** section).

Method
1 Hand out the Briefing sheets – one copy for each participant, perhaps marking the Briefing sheets to divide the participants into random groups. The ideal size for a group is four, but Delta's card is optional as it repeats information on some of the other cards. With six participants, there could be two groups of three or one group of six, with two participants sharing roles with someone else.

2 If there are several groups, discuss the question of what should happen if a group dies early. Should they start again or replace one or two Room cards in the pack and turn the clock back for a couple of hours to a point where they are still alive? Alternatively, should they stay dead and, as ghosts, lay out all the Room cards and hold a private debriefing?

3 Have a table or flat surface (even the floor) for each group. Keep the groups well separated to avoid espionage or accidental glances at the Room cards laid out by other groups.

4 Hand out to each group the 17-hour schedule and the card for Room A. Hand out (at random) the Information cards to the individual Space officers.

5 Hand out the scrap paper. Retrieve all the Briefing sheets. Set a time limit if desirable.

6 Normally a participant from a group would come to you and request a card, say, 'Room J, please'. If you keep the packs yourself, separate them on your table according to the geographical placement of the groups in order to avoid mixing one pack with another. If you want each group to service itself, you could write the letters on the backs of the cards. It is my experience that when a group has its own pack of cards face down on its own table its members do not cheat by trying to look at the underside of the cards.

Debriefing

This is one of the Five simple events listed in the Introduction and the easiest way to debrief a simple event is to ask the participants to fill in the Self-assessment sheets individually and use the results as a basis for discussion. The alternative is to take a more flexible approach and tailor the debriefing according to the particular course, the type of participants and significant episodes that occurred during the action. The following questions and suggestions could be used as a guide not only for the debriefing but also as a check-list of the sorts of things you could watch for in the action itself. (See also **Running the debriefing**, Introduction.)

Did the group check that each officer communicated all the information or merely rely on four verbal summaries? How well did they work together as a team? Did their planning involve looking at all the options and working out possible consequences? Did the group plan ahead, keep up to date with the 17-hour schedule and perhaps use scrap paper to demonstrate their ideas? Was anyone in the team given a specific job – such as checking that the group did not stray too far from Red rooms or to keep the schedule up to date or to make a map of the likely territory?

Rationale

If you wish to demonstrate the rationale of the simulation set out the whole 26 Room cards and concentrate in turn on rooms A, C, X, L, I, M and F.

Room A

Did they consider that J might be the only immunity room? If they go to J and retrace their steps to C, they would be immune *and* assured of food, whereas if they go first to C and *then* go to J, they would be immune but *not* assured of food.

Room C

Going forwards tends to maximize potential new information as they would then have the chance to learn about three new rooms (forward and at each side) whereas if they turn at right angles to grey room S, they could learn about only two new rooms as they already know that Room U is grey.

Room X

The temptation here is to turn north into blue room K in order to obtain information. This is typical of several such temptations in the labyrinth. Room K can be reached *only* by crossing the point of no return, which is a bad idea when the alternative is a safe route. To go to K needlessly risks death (and entails death) and is therefore incautious. Gamma's and Delta's Information cards advise caution. Not only is there no guarantee that a red room will be adjacent to K, but there is no certainty that the information contained within it will be worth the unnecessary risk.

The reason no information about the escape route is contained in Room K is in case the participants wish to continue the simulation by replacing the K card and turning back the clock and returning as ghosts to Room X.

If participants go to K then, possibly, they are treating the event as a game and not as a survival test – hence the reminder in room K that the event is not a game and that gamesters are the lemmings of space. In real life it is unlikely that they would be so foolhardy and would probably take the view that where there's life there's hope. (Room P is similar to Room K – a temptation to cross the point of no return in search of information.)

Room L

Because of the wall on the north side, the learning potential of going forward is the same as going at right angles to D. However, there is no good reason for changing the useful strategy of going forwards.

Room I

If they did not visit J, going to R is essential. If they went to J, going to E continues the forwards strategy and the prevailing grey, red, grey sequence and is consistent with Beta's information that going to a second immunity room is without extra value.

Room M

Room F should be visited because information could be (and is) invaluable. Room F is the first and only room where information can be obtained without fatally passing the point of no return. To go to Room T is safe, but eats up precious time.

Room F

The information is in the form of an order and should be obeyed. In any case it makes sense to assume that the designers of the labyrinth would not order a space crew to its death. The labyrinth is a test of ability, not a game of Russian Roulette.

Solution

The sensible decisions on leaving A are:

J, A, C, X, L, V, Y, N, I, E, M, F, M, Q, Z

taking 15 hours and passing with honours. See also **Author's choice**, Introduction, for further discussion of the event.

In this simulation you are Space officers Alpha, Beta, Gamma and Delta. You are at the Space School on the planet Test taking part in a 'live bullet' course. You are about to enter the final test, the labyrinth. Failure to escape from the labyrinth means death to the whole team, even though failure may have been due to lack of cooperation from just one of its members.

You will each receive an Information card. The group will also receive a 17-hour schedule and a Room card showing Room A. Place the Room card in the centre of the table and, when you decide which way to go (east, west or south), you must ask for another card by its identifying letter. When you receive this second card, place it on the table touching card A on the appropriate side and gradually build up a map of your path through the labyrinth.

Place a small coin or some other token on the card of the room you occupy and move the token as you move from room to room. This will help you keep track of your position. It will also help you to fill in the 17-hour schedule accurately. It will help you to survive.

The Information cards will not tell you that failure to fill in the 17-hour schedule properly means that you have failed the test. The reason is that the warning has so far been unnecessary as no team inefficient enough to have neglected filling in the schedule has ever come out of the labyrinth alive.

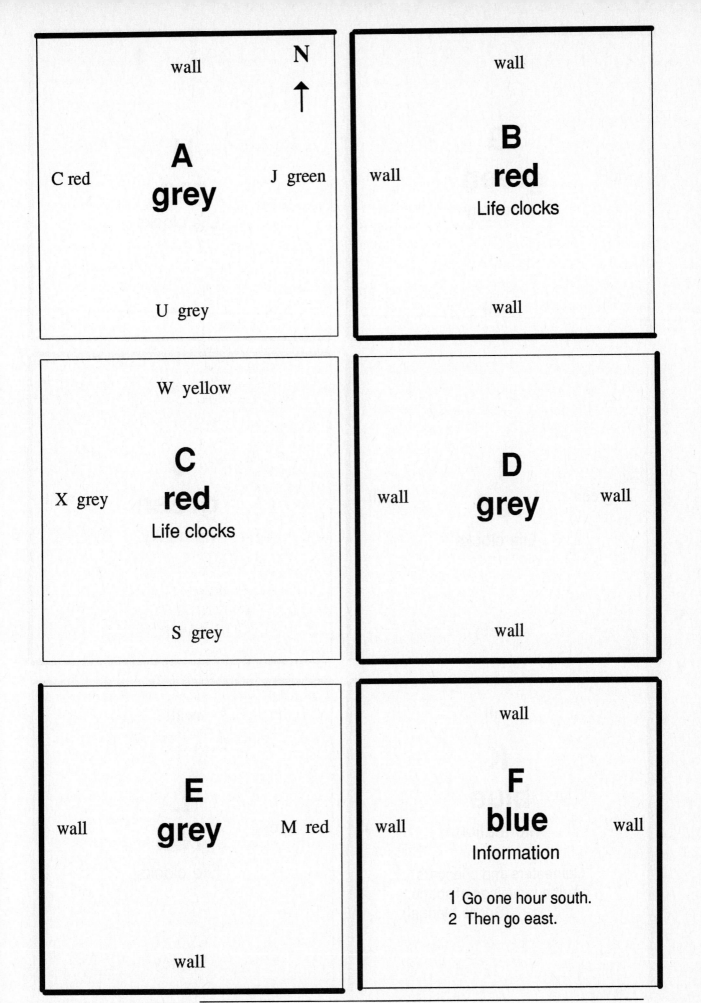

N ↑

A grey
wall
C red
J green
U grey

B red
Life clocks
wall
wall
wall

C red
Life clocks
W yellow
X grey
S grey

D grey
wall
wall
wall

E grey
wall
M red
wall

F blue
Information
wall
wall
wall

1 Go one hour south.
2 Then go east.

G
green
Immunity

wall wall

wall

H
red
Life clocks

wall

wall

wall

I
red
Life clocks

R green wall

E grey

J
green
Immunity

wall

wall

wall

K
blue
Information

wall

wall wall

'Gamesters and chancers
are the lemmings of space.'
(Space Manual)

L
red
Life clocks

wall

V grey

D grey

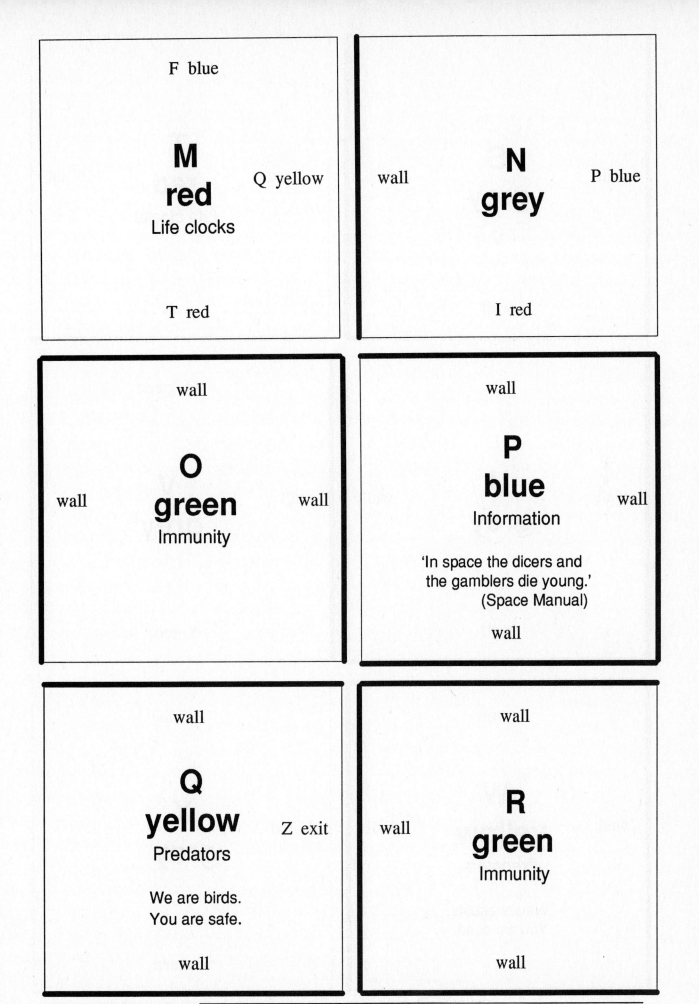

F blue

**M
red**

Q yellow

Life clocks

T red

wall

**N
grey**

P blue

I red

wall

wall

**O
green**

wall

Immunity

wall

**P
blue**

wall

Information

'In space the dicers and
the gamblers die young.'
(Space Manual)

wall

wall

**Q
yellow**

Z exit

Predators

We are birds.
You are safe.

wall

wall

**R
green**

wall

Immunity

wall

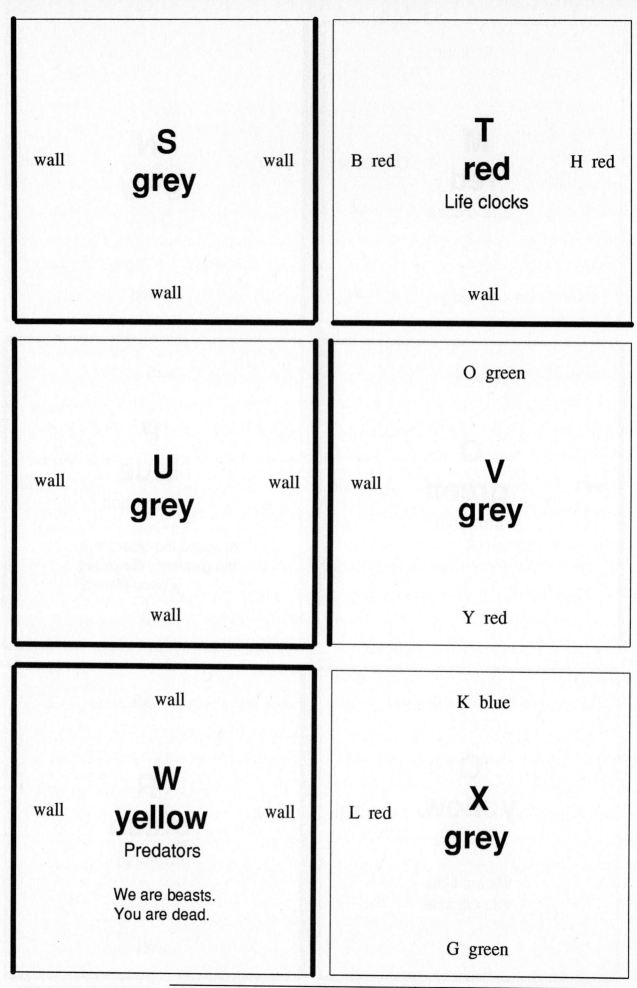

wall

S
grey

wall

wall

B red

T
red

H red

Life clocks

wall

wall

U
grey

wall

wall

O green

wall

V
grey

Y red

wall

wall

W
yellow

wall

Predators

We are beasts.
You are dead.

K blue

L red

X
grey

G green

wall **Y**
red
wall

Life clocks

N grey

Z
exit
Well done!

If this is the 15th hour
and if you visited J and F,
you pass with honours.

Officer Alpha   *Information card*

You cannot separate. You must stick together.
You start in room A. Other rooms are
allocated letters at random. Z is not a room, it
is the exit. Inside each room the doors give
information about the letter and colour of the
room beyond the door. It takes one hour to
move from one room to another. If you arrive
at Z within 17 hours you survive, otherwise
you are dead.

Once an hour you can move in any direction –
except through a wall. Grey rooms contain
nothing.

Officer Beta   *Information card*

Red rooms contain life clocks. You need a life
clock within the first three hours or you are
dead. Each life clock runs for three hours
only, and starts from the moment you pick it
up. When your last three-hour life clock stops
you are dead – there is no fourth hour.
Radiation starts on the ninth hour. Green
rooms give immunity from radiation. You
must enter a green room during the first eight
hours or you are dead. Once you have visited
a green room there is no need to visit another.

Officer Gamma   *Information card*

Blue rooms contain information, but nothing
else. Yellow rooms have predators. They
either contain birds who will let you pass or
beasts who will kill you. You must fill in the
17-hour schedule as you move hour by hour,
room by room. Hour 1 starts when you leave
room A.

This is not a game. This a test. If you think
sensibly, communicate effectively and exercise
caution, you will survive. Otherwise you die.

Officer Delta   *Information card*

You must all stick together. The map of room
A shows the north, which is a wall. To the east
is room J, which is green and will give you
immunity from radiation. To the south is room
U, which is grey and contains nothing. To the
west is room C, which is red and contains
three-hour life clocks. You need a new life
clock at least once every three hours. You
need to visit an immunity room within the first
eight hours. Hour 1 starts when you leave
room A. Exercise caution, or you die.

17-hour schedule

Hour	Room	Colour	Contents	Notes or comments
0	A	grey	empty	
1				
2				
3				
4				
5				
6				
7				
8				
9				
10				
11				
12				
13				
14				
15				
16				
17				

How did you begin? For example, did you start by discussing options or did you move out of Room A immediately someone suggested going to Room C? Did you consider that Room J might be the only immunity room in the labyrinth and that if you went first to Room C you would not be able to get to J and return safely to C?

Did you summarize what was on your Information card or did you read it out or show it to the others? If you summarized it, did anyone check to see if you had missed anything?

Did you allocate different jobs? For example, did you make someone the boss? Did you put someone in charge of keeping an eye on the time factor? Did you use the scrap paper?

Did you realize that to go forward would usually give you more information (in front and on two sides) than to turn to the right or the left as you already knew what was on one side?

Did anyone treat the event as a game and, if so, what resulted from this attitude?

How do you assess yourself?

Skills	Poor	Fair	Good	Excellent
Efficiency				
Communication				
Planning				
Team building				
Time management				
(Other)				

How do you assess your team?

Skills	Poor	Fair	Good	Excellent
Efficiency				
Communication				
Planning				
Team building				
Time management				
(Other)				

12 *Fold here*

Description This is a simulation in which groups are asked to take part in an exercise in which they have to follow instructions involving documents relating to the construction of a tower made of paper and paper-clips.

Objectives To enhance the skills of communication, problem solving, team building and time management.

Time and numbers With one group, allow half an hour. With more than one group, allow an hour because extra time is needed in the debriefing for explanations, comparisons and discussion. It is important that each group should have four participants so, if the numbers are not divisible by four, you could suggest that those left over become helpers (observers, timekeepers).

Resources
* Briefing sheet – one for each participant.
* Materials for each group:
    * instruction sheet – four copies, unfolded, in an unsealed envelope
    * roof material sheet – four copies, unfolded, in an unsealed envelope
    * tower material sheet – four copies, unfolded, in an unsealed envelope
    * base material sheet – four copies, unfolded, in an unsealed envelope
    * four paper-clips – one attached to the flap of each envelope.

Note: It is very important that the envelopes should be large enough to take the materials *unfolded* and that the envelopes should not be sealed.

* Stopwatches or watches or clocks with a second hand.
* Small tables – four people should be able to sit so that there is one at each side.
* Self-assessment sheet – one copy for each participant (see suggestions in **Debriefing** section).

Method 1 It is very important to place the correct materials in the correct envelopes before the event begins. Each table should receive a total of 16 documents. Each of the envelopes should contain (unfolded) four copies of the same sheet. Thus, one envelope will contain all four Instruction sheets, one will have all four Roof sheets, and so on. Check carefully to make sure that each envelope contains exactly four copies and that they are all the same document. It is also important that all envelopes should have one paper-clip across the flap.

2 Divide the participants at random into groups of four and seat them around separate tables as if engaged in a bridge tournament. If there are exactly 20 participants, you could either have 5 groups of 4 or 4 groups of 4 with an official Timekeeper or Observer at each table. If the numbers do *not* divide exactly by four, you can ask the extra participants to take the functions of Helpers or Timekeepers or Observers.

3 Separate the groups as far apart as possible, perhaps using screens or locating them in different rooms. The reason for this is that if groups can observe each other, one or more groups might delay starting the test until they have observed (and heard) what other groups do when they open their

envelopes. If only one room is available and tables have to be close together, you should cancel the instruction about the timing starting from the moment each group removes its first paper-clip and have everyone start together, giving them plenty of time to discuss strategy before the start.

4 Hand out the Briefing sheets – one copy to each participant. Perhaps you might draw their attention to the point in the Briefing sheet about keeping the working surfaces clear, but that participants will need a pen. Retrieve all the Briefing sheets.

5 Hand out the envelopes, one to each participant and (probably with the aid of assistants) make a written note of the time the first paper-clip is removed in each group.

Debriefing This is one of the Five simple events listed in the Introduction and the easiest way to debrief a simple event is to ask the participants to fill in the Self-assessment sheets individually and use the results as a basis for discussion. The alternative is to take a more flexible approach and tailor the debriefing according to the particular course, the type of participants and significant episodes that occurred during the action. The following questions and suggestions could be used as a guide not only for the debriefing but also as a check-list of the sorts of things you could watch for in the action itself. (See also **Running the debriefing**, Introduction.)

If there were several groups, it may be a good idea to ask them to hold a mini-debriefing and report their findings at a meeting of all the participants.

If all groups carried out their instructions and completed the task in the specified time, you can either congratulate them or ask if they had been forewarned of what would happen.

If some participants began by grabbing at the materials and folding them they will probably be defensive and seek to blame someone else, perhaps you. At this stage you could say it is not a question of blame, it is a question of learning from experience.

It may be that some participants were under the impression that the first sentence of the Briefing sheet instructed them to construct a tower. If so, you could read out the sentence to them. If they point out that the title of the simulation is 'Fold here' you can say (a) that headlines have to be short and can be misleading, (b) that there was no reason to assume that the title was an order and not a description of the type of materials and (c) that if they were in any doubt they would have been better advised to read the instructions before jumping to doubtful conclusions, particularly in view of the first instruction.

Whether they were successful or not, did they delay taking off the paper-clips in order to plan their procedures? Did they elect a leader or arrange for there to be a leader? For example, they might have decided that the first person to come across any instructions would automatically become leader. Was anyone put in charge of keeping an eye on the clock? Did they draw up any sort of contingency plans? Did anyone take off the paper-clip without consulting the others?

This is a simulation in which groups are asked to take part in an exercise in which they have to follow instructions involving documents relating to the construction of a tower made of paper and paper-clips.

You are an Applicant for a job at the Ministry of Science and are about to take part in the final test, the Group test. At the end of the morning session, the procedure for the Group test was explained by the Chief Assessment Officer, who made the following points:

* you will be sitting in groups of four around tables and your job will be to work as a team

* you are advised to clear the surface of your table of any of your own belongings – briefcases, notebooks, etc., but you will need a pen

* you will each receive an envelope containing documents relating to the construction of a model tower made of paper, consisting of base, tower and roof

* each envelope will have the flap secured with a paper-clip and it will be a timed test, which starts from the moment that a member of your team removes the first paper-clip from an envelope

* you will find instructions about what you have to do when you open your envelopes.

Instruction sheet

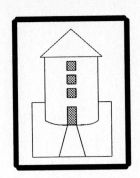

1 Read these instructions before you start.

2 The target time for the task is three minutes. A group scores ten points if the task is completed within three minutes. If completed in four minutes, the score is five points. If it takes longer than four minutes, no points are awarded. Do not neglect to read these instructions in a rush to finish the task in the quickest possible time.

3 There is a total of 16 sheets of paper in the 4 envelopes. Sort out the sheets so that each member of your team receives a complete set consisting of this Instruction sheet, the Roof material sheet, the Tower material sheet and the Base material sheet.

4 Mark the outside of each envelope for identification purposes by writing 'Red' on one envelope, 'Blue' on another, 'Yellow' on the third and 'Green' on the fourth.

5 Place in each of the four envelopes one complete set of the materials: an Instruction sheet, a Roof material sheet, a Tower material sheet and a Base material sheet. First, check to see that none of the sheets have been damaged by being folded or torn. If any of the sheets have been damaged or if any paper-clips have been damaged, the damaged materials must be placed in the envelope marked 'Green' and one penalty point will be deducted for each sheet or clip damaged.

6 Secure the flaps of as many of your envelopes as possible, using only undamaged paper-clips and place the four envelopes on the table, so that each person has an envelope in front of them.

7 The test ends at the moment the above instructions have been completed.

Roof material sheet

1 Fold outwards along the long vertical line that runs down the centre.

2 Fold outwards along the three horizontal lines.

3 Tuck in *this* flap to make the triangular shaped roof.

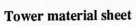 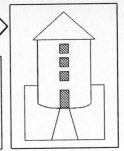

Tower material sheet

1 Partially straighten out a paper-clip to use as a skewer.
2 Bend this page round into a cylinder and secure the tower by pressing the skewer through the two holes at both ends of the page.

 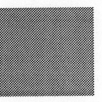  

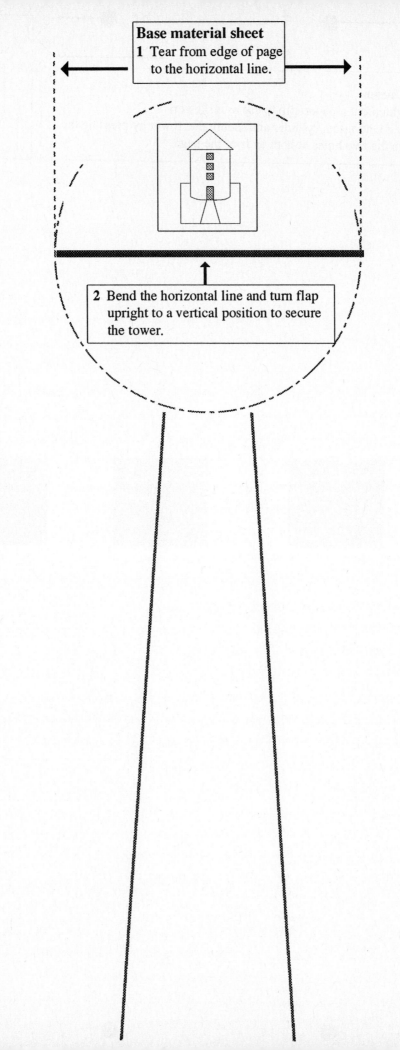

Base material sheet
1 Tear from edge of page to the horizontal line.

2 Bend the horizontal line and turn flap upright to a vertical position to secure the tower.

How did you begin? For example, did you make a decision that everyone must keep their hands off their paper-clip until the procedures had been agreed?

Did you allocate different jobs? For example, did you make someone the boss? Did you decide that the first person to find any instructions in their envelope would become the boss? Did you give someone the job of timing the operation and giving you time checks every minute or so?

How did you handle disagreements?

Did you automatically assume that you had to build a tower or did you realize that the Briefing sheet did not state that this was the case?

How do you assess yourself?

Skills	Poor	Fair	Good	Excellent
Efficiency				
Communication				
Problem solving				
Team building				
Time management				
(Other)				

How do you assess your team?

Skills	Poor	Fair	Good	Excellent
Efficiency				
Communication				
Problem solving				
Team building				
Time management				
(Other)				

13 *Houses challenge*

Description
This is a problem-solving game in which the Lords and Ladies of the Houses of Stone, Paper and Scissors can challenge each other, but first have to identify not only the other two Houses, but also their own. Each player is given a Name card, plus one of three Clue cards. The event can be run in the format of an icebreaker.

Objectives
The aim is to enhance the skills of communication and problem solving.

Time and numbers
The minimum number would be about six. With more than 20 participants you could divide them into 2 groups and run parallel events. The time required is about half an hour for one event or up to an hour for two parallel events, because of the extra time needed for explanation, comparison and discussion in the debriefing.

Resources
* Briefing sheet – one copy for each player.
* Clue cards – one for each player. (There are six Clue cards altogether).
* Name cards – one for each player.
* Meetings sheet – one for each player.
* Scrap paper.

Method
1 Depending on the numbers, cut out the Name cards and the six Clue cards. If there are more than six players, cut out as many Clue cards as participants, with roughly the same number of each card.

2 If you run the event mainly as an icebreaker you could set a time limit for each meeting and give a signal for players to change partners. If your priorities are communication and problem solving, no time limit need be set, although you could ask players to end their talk quickly if someone is waiting to meet them.

3 Hand out the Briefing sheets – one to each player. If there are more than 18 players at least 2 players will have the same name. If this is the case, tell the players that if two meet and find that they have the same name, they must merge into one player and stick together.

4 Hand out the Meetings sheets – one to each player. Place the Clue cards face down and let each participant pick their own, asking them to conceal the clues.

5 Make the scrap paper available and set whatever time limit is desirable. Retrieve the Briefing sheets.

Debriefing
Apart from perhaps determining who won the game and revealing the answers to the enigmatic clues (four, five and six), one point of interest is whether the players were frustrated by not being told the name of their own House. Ask them if they felt a sense of lost identity and how they tackled the problem.

The debriefing might look at the sociability of the players as politeness is part of the scenario. Did many players ignore this element of communication skill and simply rush from person to person trying solve the problem? Did they use a courteous, and perhaps elaborate, form of address at the start and end of each meeting? How open were the players about revealing their own Clues? If they discovered that the solution was based on anagrams, did they reveal this?

102

Solution

The solution is that the names are anagrams of flowers, fruit and animals. As stated in the Briefing sheet, the aristocratic society pays great attention to people's names. Note that the people named in the enigmatic clues (Lord Eros, Lord Groane, Lady Shore) do not appear in the game itself. If you wish to remember which House is which, a helpful mnemonic is that fruit have stones and flowers are cut with scisssors. It is less easy to connect paper with animals – perhaps a paper tiger. The answers to the anagrams are:

House of Scissors (flowers)	**House of Stone** (fruit)	**House of Paper** (animals)
Pluti (tulip	Prage (grape)	Grite (tiger)
Nupil (lupin)	Arep (pear)	Phese (sheep)
Dichor (orchid)	Viole (olive)	Woc (cow)
Roccsu (crocus)	Chape (peach)	Nilo (lion)
Faddolfi (daffodil)	Pleap (apple)	Snobi (bison)
Yasid (daisy)	Teda (date)	Clame (camel)

The answers to the three enigmatic Clues (four, five and six) are:

* Lord Eros of Scissors: Eros = rose, roses have thorns – thorny problems
* Lord Groane of Stone: Groane = orange, orange is a colour – colourful character
* Lady Shore of Paper: Shore = horse, horses live in stables – Lady Shore has stables.

This is a problem-solving game in which the Lords and Ladies of the Houses of Stone, Paper and Scissors can challenge each other on the basis that Stone wins against Scissors, Scissors wins against Paper and Paper wins against Stone. It is an aristocratic society that pays great attention to people's names.

You will receive a Name card, which you should display, plus a Clue card, which you can either keep secret or reveal, You will also have a Meetings sheet on which to record the names of the people you meet and whether any challenge is issued.

The problem is not only to identify the House of the person you are meeting, but also the name of your own House. If you feel confident enough to make a challenge, you should utter the formal words, 'I give you my challenge' and, if you are challenged, you say, 'I accept your challenge'. No one should try to explain why a challenge has been made or record the result of the challenge, which can be worked out at the end of the game. Points are scored as follows:

	Challenger	Challenged
Challenger wins	1	0
Challenger loses	0	1
Challenge to member of own House	-2	2

The reason you lose two points if you inadvertently challenge a member of your own House is that such a challenge is embarrassing in courtly etiquette.

By tradition, the Lords and Ladies find the courtesy and pleasure of the meetings more important than point scoring, although embarrassments tend to be remembered. The scores are written down officially only at the end of the event, should anyone wish to do so. Your job is to meet people in pairs (not in threes, or more) in a courtly and friendly manner and to try to solve the problem.

Lords and Ladies of the House of Paper like animals.

Lords and Ladies of the House of Scissors like flowers.

Lords and Ladies of the House of Stone like fruit.

Lord Groane of the House of Stone is a keen rock climber.
He likes fruit. He is a colourful character.

Lord Eros of the House of Scissors is a keen archer.
He likes flowers. His pointed arrows cause thorny problems.

Lady Shore of the House of Paper is a writer.
She likes animals. She has a fine mansion with excellent stables.

Pluti	Prage	Grite
Nupil	Arep	Phese
Dichor	Viole	Woc
Roccsu	Chape	Nilo
Faddolfi	Pleap	Snobi
Yasid	Teda	Clame

(Flowers)	(Fruits)	(Animals)

106

Meetings sheet

Name:

I met	Any challenge	Any comments

14 *Into Green and Care*

Description A simulation about a woman who has inherited her late husband's business – the Green Garden and Care Company – and has decided to manage it with the help of her family. This simulation has a hidden agenda.

Objectives To enhance the skills of communication, diplomacy and planning.

Time and numbers Each Family should number about four. The time taken will probably be about 20 minutes if there is one Family only and if the Family does not request the Factsheet for the Human Care division. With more Families, and with Families who request the Factsheets, the event could last an hour and a half because of the extra time needed in the debriefing for explanations, comparisons and discussion.

Resources
* Briefing sheet – one for each participant.
* Letter from Mrs Smith – one for each Family.
* Letter of reply from Mrs Robinson – one for each Family.
* Two Factsheets (Green Garden division and Human Care division) – to be handed out only if the whole team stands up for one minute for each Factsheet (see Briefing sheet).
* Headed notepaper for each Family.
* Separate tables for each Family, as far apart as possible.
* Scrap paper.

Method
1 Hand out the Briefing sheets – one to each participant.

2 Divide the participants into 'Families' of about three or four people, with as much space between the groups as possible.

3 Retrieve the Briefing sheets and hand out the Letter from Mrs Smith and the Letter of reply from Mrs Robinson, plus the Headed notepaper – one copy of each to each Family.

4 Do not, of course, hand out the two Factsheets. Keep these in a place of security and where they cannot be observed by inquisitive passing participants.

5 If a Family reaches its decision far earlier than the others without having requested the Factsheet for the Human Care division, you could, if you wish, extend the simulation for them by saying that the editor of the local newspaper has just telephoned, saying that the paper is about to publish a story with the headline 'Widow sells manacles and whips'. The editor asks whether Mrs Smith (and Family) would like to make any comments that could be added to the story.

Note: Should a Family express a wish to telephone Mrs Robinson then you have the option of taking on that role for the purpose of the phone call, in which case be helpful, friendly and cautious about saying too much over the telephone. Do not playact the role – behave professionally.

Debriefing If there were several Family groups, it could be a good idea to ask the groups to debrief themselves, making available the two Factsheets to any groups that did not request them.

The hidden agenda in this simulation is that things are not what they seem because the Human Care division is less than explicit about its products, presumably to avoid embarrassing publicity.

How long did it take the Families to realize that something might be amiss and what was it that rang the alarm bell? The wording of the two letters can be analysed. Did the Families realize that Mrs Smith's question about what the company 'actually manufactures' was evaded in Mrs Robinson's reply by (a) making a technical distinction between 'manufacture' and 'assemble' and (b) treating the sprinkler question as if it was a specific question rather than an example of the sort of information required about the company's range. Did the participants notice that although Mrs Robinson stated that the Implements department of the Green Garden division referred to garden tools, she did not say what the Human Care division produced, nor give any examples of what was assembled by either the Guardian Aids department or the Traditional Applications department? Were suspicions lulled by the emotive words 'green' and 'care'?

If the participants had been in the position of Mrs Robinson, how would they have replied to Mrs Smith's original letter? If the Families used the Headed notepaper to respond to Mrs Robinson's letter, how effective was this in terms of communication and diplomacy?

Whether or not the Families discovered the true situation, how effective was their planning? Did they draw up any lists of things to do or check? Did they make any plans to visit the Company?

Regarding the methodology of the event, did they find the hidden agenda objectionable and think they had been unfairly manipulated or tricked?

This is a simulation about a woman who has inherited her late husband's business, the Green Garden and Care Company, and has decided to manage it with the help of her Family. The Family support each other and there are no feuds, so treat the situation as if you were a member of a committee that cooperates well.

You will have copies of the Letter from Mrs Smith to the Manager of Green Garden and Care Company, Mrs Rita Robinson, and the Letter of reply from Mrs Robinson regarding possible reorganization of the Company. This reply mentions two Factsheets that are available. If you think either would be of any use in making your decisions, you must indicate the effort required to obtain them by the whole Family standing up for a period of one minute for each Factsheet you request. If you agree to the proposed reorganization, write 'OK' at the top of Mrs Robinson's letter and add all your signatures. If you wish to take other action, you should write a letter to Mrs Robinson on your Headed notepaper.

Dear Mrs Robinson,

Following our discussion on the telephone about whether
or not I should sell Green Garden and Care Company or
become Managing Director, I have decided to try to run
the Company and see how it goes. I shall have the
support of my family.

As you know, my late husband told us nothing about the
business, so could you let me know its financial
prospects (this is very important to me) and also tell
me what it is that the Company actually manufactures -
do you make lawn sprinklers for example? Also, you
mentioned a crucial decision that I might have to face
if I took over. What is it?

Yours,

(Mrs Dawn Smith)

Green Garden and Care Company

Dear Mrs Smith,

May I say how pleased I am that you have decided not to sell the business and I am glad that you will have the support of your family. I appreciate your concern that your late husband did not discuss the business with you or your family, but, as I said in our chat, it was so well organized by your late husband that it virtually runs itself.

Regarding manufacture, we manufacture nothing ourselves, but assemble and finish products made by sub-contractors. We do assemble lawn sprinklers, the sprinkler is made by one sub-contractor and the hose by another.

None of our products are available to the general public. The Green Garden division sells direct to businesses and corporations, while the Human Care division sells exclusively to government departments and agencies. If you would like more detailed information about the products in our range, please let me know and I will send you our Factsheet for the Green Garden division and/or the Factsheet for the Human Care division.

The crucial question of reorganization is whether to phase out the loss-making Implements department (garden tools). Here are the figures for last year and the previous year (profits before taxation).

	Last year	Previous year
Green Garden division		
* Lawn Care department	57 342	55 474
* Implements department	-5 011	-302
Human Care division		
* Guardian Aids department	891 521	845 225
* Traditional Applications department	87 334	86 623
Total profit	1 031 186	987 020

Although nothing was definitely decided, your husband thought it might be a good idea to phase out the Implements department over a period of about 12 months and to expand the Human Care division, which would mean there would be no staff redundancies. If you agree to this reorganization, perhaps you could follow your husband's practice and simply write 'OK' on the top of this letter and add your signature.

If, on the other hand, you prefer another course of action or perhaps wish to leave matters as they are, please drop me a line. Naturally, I should be most happy to discuss any matter with you and your family at any time.

Rita Robinson

Factsheet 1: Green Garden division

* We cater only for privileged customers – businesses, corporations and institutions – guaranteeing a high quality of products, service and advice.

* Our Lawn Care department is devoted exclusively to the establishment and maintenance of healthy lawns, including the tools required – lawn sprinklers, mowing machines, etc.

* Our Implements department supports high-quality general purpose garden tools – spades, hoes, forks and all are suitable for work that can be in the public eye.

Factsheet 2:   Human Care division

Guardian Aids department

* These consist of high-quality merchandise, finished by our craft workshop to reliable standards so that they are suitable in all climates.

* We sell to 38 governments, many in the Third World, and we have no customers in the private sector.

* Our products have a particular appeal in these days of concern about human rights and prison reform, since our aim is to provide humane but secure guardianship.

Traditional Applications department

* We supply to governments whose traditional culture and penal system requires the use of traditional implements. These can be purchased direct from our catalogue. They are regulation implements including batons.

Visitors

* We welcome visitors from penal institutions and we provide demonstrations of the efficacy of all our equipment, including locks, chains, manacles and other security devices and implements.

15 *Number auction*

Description This is an exercise in which 4 teams, each with 14 dollars, take part in an auction of 5 numbers. The numbers will later be valued according to given specifications.

Objectives To enhance the skills of problem solving, team building and time management.

Time and numbers The event will probably last for about an hour. If the participants are not afraid of arithmetic, the minimum number is four, with each team consisting of one person. If the participants are average ability it is better to set the minimum at eight, with two in each team, and better still to have three or four in each team. With 20 or more participants, consider running the simulation as 2 (or more) separate events and allow about an hour and a half because of the extra time needed in the debriefing for explanations, comparisons and discussion.

Resources
* Briefing sheet – one copy for each participant.
* Number cards – one copy of each for the Auctioneer.
* Scrap paper.

Method
1 Arrange the furniture to facilitate the action. In the planning period the teams should be widely separated, but in the auction the teams should be seated in a semi-circle facing the Auctioneer.

2 Decide who should be the Auctioneer – yourself or a participant. Fix a time for the start of the auction. This should probably be 15-30 minutes after you have handed out the Briefing sheets and scrap paper. The reason for allowing a generous amount of time is that although the arithmetical values can be worked out in a few minutes, it takes longer to work out a suitable bidding strategy because the numbers will be auctioned in a random order.

3 Hand out the Briefing sheets – one copy to each participant. Hand out the scrap paper. Allow teams to keep their Briefing sheets as this is the only document containing the rules of the auction.

4 Start the auction by shuffling the five Number cards, face down. Then hold up the top card and ask for bids for that number. Continue with the other four cards.

5 Although the teams will probably keep a record of the bids, it might be a good idea for you (whether you are the Auctioneer or not) to write down the result of each bid in a three-column table – the headings being the number, the team and the dollars.

Debriefing Observing teams tackle the numerical part can be very interesting. Sometimes an attempt will be made to divide the labour – 'You count up the ones, I'll do the twos'. Someone might object that this means counting the same sums twice over. Someone else might say that that does not matter as both 2+1 and 1+2 are eligible. The arithmetic is easy; it is the unusual nature of the task that causes uncertainty. One question in the debriefing would be whether the winning team contained the best mathematicians or the best 'streetwise' problem solvers.

The obvious starting point is the 'official' value of each number, which is that number 1 is worth $8 dollars, number 2 is worth $14, numbers 3 and 4 are each worth $12 and number 5 is worth $10.

Number	Multiplication	Addition	Dollars
1	(none)	1+2 2+1, 1+3 3+1, 1+4 4+1, 1+5 5+1	8
2	2x3 3x2, 2x4 4x2, 2x5 5x2	2+1 1+2, 2+3 3+2, 2+4 4+2, 2+5 5+2	14
3	3x2 2x3, 3x4 4x3	3+1 1+3, 3+2 2+3, 3+4 4+3, 3+5 5+3	12
4	4x2 2x4, 4x3 3x4	4+1 1+4, 4+2 2+4, 4+3 3+4. 4+5 5+4	12
5	5x2 2x5	5+1 1+5, 5+2 2+5, 5+3 3+5, 5+4 4+5	10
			56

A point to note is that the the total dollar value of 56 for the 5 numbers is exactly equal to the money the 4 teams start with – 4 x14 dollars. If there is a 'best' strategy it is too complicated to work out in the time available as it would depend on the order in which the numbers were auctioned. However, a practical strategy is to keep track not only of what one's own team has spent and has left, but also how much the other teams have spent and have left. An unlikely but clear cut example is to suppose that teams A, B and C bought numbers 2, 3 and 4 for $1 less than the official price, each making a profit of $1. This would allow team D to buy numbers 1 and 5 for only $4 each (as no other team would have more than $3 left), allowing team D to finish with two numbers worth $18, plus $6 in cash, thus making a total of $24 in assets and thus making a profit of $10.

As well as the problem solving aspect, the debriefing is likely to cover team building and time management. Did they elect a leader? How did they choose the bidder? How did they arrange communication between the bidder and the rest of the team? Was the bidder in charge of the timing – when and when not to bid? What did they think of their own strategies compared with the strategies of other teams? Would they behave differently if the auction were rerun?

This is an exercise in which 4 teams, each with $14, take part in an auction of 5 numbers. The numbers are later valued according to given specifications.

Numbers to be auctioned are 1-5 and these will be auctioned in random order. Each team has $14 that it may use for purchasing 1 or more of these 5 numbers. There is no physical money – the purchases are book transactions and the dollars are not real dollars. (Do not substutite real money as this adds little or nothing to the realism and it can cause bitter argument and resentment later.)

Each team must operate independently. Collaboration between teams is not permitted. Only one person in each team is allowed to make bids at the auction, although there can be consultations or instructions.

At the end of the event the facilitator will produce the 'official' dollar value of each of the five numbers. This will be used to determine which team has the highest value of assets – the official value of the numbers plus any cash left in hand. This means that if a team has made no purchases, its assets will be $14.

The official value of each of the five numbers will be measured according to the number of times it can be used with one of the other four figures in simple sums of addition and multiplication in which:

* the answer is not more than 12
* the answer itself is not counted as part of the value
* a sum can be counted twice by being reversed
* none of the numbers can be repeated, and that includes the answer.

The following examples may help explain these rules.

The sum 2+3=5 would mean that 2 is worth $1 in that sum, 3 is worth $1 in that sum and 5 is worth nothing because it is the answer. The sum can be reversed and counted again, thus 3+2=5 is also eligible.

Not allowed are:

* 5x1=5, because two of the numbers are the same
* 4+4=8, because two of the numbers are the same
* 3x5=15, because the total is more than 12
* 5-2=3, because only addition and multiplication are allowed
* 1+2+3=6, because only two numbers can be added or multiplied in each sum.

16 *Whistlers and movers*

Description   A simulation in which three teams, each containing a Whistler and several Movers, have the job of getting blindfolded Movers into a particular part of the room, the event taking place at the Selection and Training Centre of Naval Intelligence.

Objectives   To enhance the skills of communication, negotiation, planning and problem solving.

Time and numbers   The event will probably take one to two hours. The minimum number is seven, which would mean three teams consisting of one Whistler and one Mover, and a team of one representing the Psychologists and Trainers of the Selection and Training Centre. With 18 participants there could be a Naval team of 3 and 3 teams each consisting of a Whistler and 4 Movers.

Resources

* Briefing sheet – one copy for each participant.
* Instructions to Whistlers and Movers – one copy to each team, including the
* Naval team.
* Sufficient safe space.
* Whistles (or some substitute) for the three Whistlers.
* Blindfolds for the Movers.
* Scrap paper.
* Possibly coloured notices or labels for the red, blue and green bases and target areas.

Method

1 Before the simulation begins, you must decide on two vital points. One is the whistle question. Probably the ideal is three identical whistles with a single note. This would encourage teams to cooperate, otherwise competitive whistling of the same note would be chaotic. Far less difficult would be musical type whistles on which Whistlers could play coded signals. If no whistles are obtainable or if there is a danger of the whistling disturbing other classes, an alternative would be to provide a spoon and glass and turn the Whistlers into Tinklers. The other important point concerns the furniture. You do not want Movers tripping over chairs, tables and so on and hurting themselves. If a clear space cannot be provided, look for other options, for example, a room of suitable size that does not have much furniture (such as a hall or gym) or run the event in the open air.

2 Before you hand out the Briefing sheets, mark a few of them with the letter N to indicate who are the members of the Naval team, place them face down on the table and ask the participants to pick their own.

3 Set a time limit for the start of the debriefing. Warn the participants of any special restrictions ('Don't blow too loudly', 'Keep the Movers away from this sharp edge').

4 Retrieve the Briefing sheets. Move the candidates to a 'waiting room' area and the Naval team to an 'office' area and give all the documents, whistles, blindfolds and scrap paper to the Naval team.

5 If the Naval team does not do it straight away, insist that they meet the candidates and hand out the Instructions. This avoids the candidates hanging around and feeling neglected.

Debriefing

The debriefing will probably start at the point where the event finished – the remarks made by the Naval team.

The format could be a mini-debriefing within teams and perhaps ask them to respond to specific questions, such as, would they do it any differently with hindsight and which aspect was the most (a) interesting (b) unpleasant and (c) revealing.

Did the teams negotiate with each other? What did the Naval team think of the applicants (which might be different from their comments made within the event) and what did the applicants think of the Naval team? Did the whistle codes include a signal to 'come to me' or 'hold each other in line behind a leading Mover', etc., or were the codes simply basic 'right, left, forward, stop' commands?

To what extent was the exercise likely to help in the selection of candidates for Naval Intelligence (or for business management or for running a youth club)?

This is a simulation in which three teams, each containing a Whistler and several Movers, have the job of getting blindfolded Movers into a particular part of the room, the event taking place at the Selection and Training Centre of Naval Intelligence.

You are either Naval officers (trainers and psychologists) at the Centre or you are candidates who have applied for a job in Naval Intelligence. For the last two days the candidates have undergone various tests, watched and assessed by the trainers and psychologists.

Today is the Group test, entitled Whistlers and movers.

The simulation begins with all the candidates in a waiting room and the Naval team in their office. Almost immediately the Naval team will visit the candidates, divide them at random into three teams (Red team, Blue team, Green team), and hand out the Instructions to Whistlers and Movers.

Instructions to Whistlers and Movers

From: Naval Assessment Staff
To: Candidates in the Whistlers and movers exercise

Read these instructions individually and in silence. Do not communicate with other members of your team or with other teams until we announce that the discussion period has begun.

During the discussion period you can plan how to code your whistle signals and you will be able to practise. You can visit other teams for the purpose of coordination and cooperation of the whistling arrangements, but only one member of each team can be absent from the team's base at any one time. Some time during the discussion period you must select a member of your team to be your Whistler.

At the end of the discussion period we will indicate the area that must be occupied by all three Whistlers, who must stay together in this area. The Movers will be blindfolded in the centre of the room and moved to random and well separated positions. We will then mark out the Red, Blue and Green target areas.

Apart from the whistling, candidates must remain silent until we announce that the exercise is ended and that blindfolds can be removed.

The scoring system is as follows:

* Red team: two points for each Red Mover reaching the Red target area; one point for each Blue Mover reaching the Blue target area

* Blue team: two points for each Blue Mover reaching the Blue target area; one point for each Green Mover reaching the Green target area

* Green team: two points for each Green Mover reaching the Green target area; one point for each Red Mover reaching the Red target area.

Your scores will play a part, but only a small part, in our overall assessment of your suitability for a job in Naval Intelligence.

Naval team

Immediately and now:

1 visit the candidates and divide them into three teams at random
2 separate the teams as far apart as possible
3 give each candidate a copy of the Instructions.

In five minutes:

4 announce the start of the discussion period and say how long it will last
5 hand out scrap paper, whistles and blindfolds so that the teams can practise
6 indicate the Whistlers' area and the three target areas, but do not label them Red, Blue and Green at this stage.

After the end of the discussion period:

7 blindfold the Movers and place them in position
8 identify the target areas as Red, Blue and Green
9 start exercise and observe
10 end exercise and remove blindfolds.

After the end of the whistling exercise:

11 thank the groups for their cooperation and congratulate them on their efforts
12 report a few observations (not judgements) relating to each team's planning
13 remind the candidates that the results of the tests will depend on careful assessment and discussion by yourselves and that the candidates should hear the decision within two weeks.

Personal areas

17 *Afterwards*

Description

In this simulation the participants have the roles of four Managers dealing with hypotheticals, strategies, positives and negatives and tackle the problem of how the lessons of the course could be applied back at work. In the debriefing the real situation can be discussed in the light of the suggestions and strategies arising from the hypotheticals (imaginary situations).

Objectives

To enhance the skills of communication, counselling and planning.

Time and numbers

About two hours should be allowed, assuming a lengthy debriefing. However, if only the hypothetical cases are discussed, the event will probably last for about an hour. The minimum number is four. There is no maximum.

Resources

* Briefing sheet – one copy for each participant.
* Managerial responsibility cards – a set of four for each group.
* Hypotheticals form – one for each participant.
* Scrap paper.

Method

1 The event does not envisage four people sitting around a table, apart from the final ten minutes. For most of the event the four in each team will meet as pairs and this can affect the way the furniture is arranged.

2 Hand out the Briefing sheets – one to each participant – perhaps marking the sheets to divide the participants at random into groups of four. If the total number does not divide evenly by four, you could have Helpers (Observers, Reporters). Allocate at random the four managerial jobs – Positives, Negatives, Hypotheticals and Strategies – perhaps putting the Managerial responsibility cards face down and allowing the participants to pick their own.

3 Make the scrap paper available. Retrieve the Briefing sheets. Fix a time for the start of the ten-minute joint meeting of the four Managers that concludes the simulation.

4 Ask the participants to divide into two pairs – Positive and Negative Managers and Hypotheticals and Strategies Managers – to start the meetings as explained in the Briefing sheet.

Debriefing

The debriefing will probably start by establishing what happened in the groups. How well did the participants work together and support each other in their different areas of responsibility? How well did they communicate? How effective was the counselling in the hypothetical cases? Were the planning strategies useful? Did anyone try to dominate the proceedings by taking over other people's duties?

The debriefing will probably move from hypothetical cases to real and personal cases. Can the participants use the same thought processes to (a) cover a variety of options, (b) achieve a balance between overoptimism and overpessimism and (c) judge which strategies are likely to yield the best results in the real and specific situations?

This simulation is about imaginary examples – hypotheticals. You are four Managers responsible for the departments of Hypotheticals, Strategies, Positives and Negatives and you tackle the problem of how the lessons of a course could be applied back at work in an imaginary situation involving at least two people. Each Manager will receive a Managerial responsibility card and you may show these cards to your colleagues if you wish to do so.

To allow for a full exchange of ideas and options, all meetings except the final one must be between pairs. The first meetings must be between the Managers of the Positives and Negatives and between the Managers of the Hypotheticals and Strategies. You should explain and discuss your managerial functions and the job boundaries, leaving hypothetical cases to later meetings. Subsequent meetings should rotate, with you meeting in turn the other three Managers to discuss hypothetical cases.

If one meeting has split up and the Managers are waiting for you to finish, wind up your discussion quickly. At each meeting give a brief description of what was discussed at the meeting you have just completed.

The final ten minutes of the event is a joint meeting of all four Managers to try to reach conclusions and agree on recommendations.

You will each receive a Hypotheticals form to record the hypothetical cases and make comments.

Department of Hypotheticals

It is your responsibility to invent hypothetical situations (imaginary examples of someone returning to work after a course), which must involve more than one person. Thus, a hypothetical about a person trying to boost their own self-confidence is permitted only if the hypothesis envisages another person who helps or hinders. Each hypothetical does not have to be completely different from the previous one, it can be a modification by changing one or more aspects – a person's age, sex, race, personality, position in the hierarchy and so on.

Although you must not try to take over another Manager's responsibilities, you are free to make suggestions to that Manager. You can show this card to other Managers.

Department of Strategies

It is your responsibility to suggest strategies for the imaginary people in the hypothetical situations. The strategies do not have to be the 'best' strategies. A poor strategy or an extreme strategy can sometimes produce the greatest illumination and learning. A strategy can be adopted as part of a hypothetical if the Manager of Hypotheticals agrees.

Although you must not try to take over another Manager's responsibilities, you are free to make suggestions to that Manager. You can show this card to other Managers.

Department of Positives

It is your responsibility to put forward possible positive outcomes from the imaginary strategies in the hypothetical situations. The aim is not to argue in favour of the strategies but merely to list as many favourable outcomes as possible.

Although you must not try to take over another Manager's responsibilities, you are free to make suggestions to that Manager. You can show this card to other Managers.

Department of Negatives

It is your responsibility to put forward possible negative outcomes from the imaginary strategies in the hypothetical situations. The aim is not to argue against the strategies but merely to list as many unfavourable outcomes as possible.

Although you must not try to take over another Manager's responsibilities, you are free to make suggestions to that Manager. You can show this card to other Managers.

Hypotheticals form

Name:

Department:

Case facts	Positives and negatives	Suggestions

18 *Cosmetic friends*

Description   This is a simulation in which a cosmetics manufacturing company has suffered from an unduly high number of disruptive short-term office romances and a confidential report by a psychologist attributes this to the new office decor, which has acted as a temporary but relatively powerful aphrodisiac that has affected females.

Objectives   To enhance the skills of communication, planning and team building in a context involving gender.

Time and numbers   The event should take between half an hour and an hour, depending on whether anyone realizes the marketing potential of the discovery. The minimum number is four. There is no maximum because the simulation could be run as separate but parallel events. There are roles for six within a management team, but this can be reduced to four if necessary.

Resources
* Enough space to ensure privacy between groups, otherwise overheard remarks could reveal useful ideas.
* Briefing sheet – one for each participant.
* Psychologist's report – one for each participant.
* Job tag sheet – one sheet for each group.
* Scrap paper.

Method
1 If there are more than eight participants, divide them into separate groups at random, perhaps by marking the Briefing sheets. Allocate at random the Job tags for the six departmental heads. With groups of four or five, drop one or two of the Job tags, but not that of Personnel Manager.

2 Do not, of course, mention the possibility that the aphrodisiac effect might be valuable and marketable or hint that the participants should look at the problem from all possible angles.

3 Ask the participants in each group to separate to indicate that they are alone in their offices. Hand out copies of the Psychologist's report – one to each participant. Make the scrap paper available.

4 Retrieve all copies of the Briefing sheets and set a time for the meeting to start. Probably only five minutes contemplation time is needed.

Debriefing   If there are several groups, the debriefing could start with a series of mini-debriefings in which each group debriefs itself and then reports the findings to the other groups.

Communication skills in this event can be assessed by interactions. How well did each group cooperate and communicate? If one person said very little, what was the reaction of the others? A logical consequence of the scenario is that the Personnel Manager should take the chair. Did this happen? Before they started discussing matters of substance, did they set up any procedure to enhance communication – for example by deciding to begin the meeting by going round the table to get reactions to the Psychologist's report?

A key question is whether the participants accepted the outline for action as contained in the Psychologist's report or whether they looked at other possibilities, particularly the exploitation of the aphrodisiac effect in some way. If this was considered, did the plans cover such crucial issues as confidentiality, the legal position, the potential markets? Did they consider the export market? Did the plans include consulting experts in various fields?

Did they discuss the position of the owner? Did they forget about her? They knew from the Briefing sheet that she wished to be informed on matters of importance and had requested a report on options and recommendations in such circumstances. Was their attitude, whatever it was, influenced in any way by the fact that the owner was a woman?

At the end of the meeting was there any summing up? Did they write down any recommendations or list the options?

This is a simulation in which a cosmetics manufacturing company has suffered from an unduly high number of disruptive short-term office romances and a confidential Report by a psychologist attributes this to the new office decor, which has acted as a temporary but relatively powerful aphrodisiac that has affected females.

You are a Manager at Care Cosmetic Company. There are six Managers and their departments are Administration, Finance, Personnel, Production, Research and Sales. You are based at their Head Office where staff number about 150, but the manufacture of the cosmetics takes place at a factory out of town.

The owner of Care Cosmetic Company does not attend the monthly management meetings. She wishes to be informed of company business only if it is a matter of importance and, in that case, she requires a statement of options and recommendations.

The monthly meetings are fairly informal. The chair is taken by the Manager of the department that is most affected by the question being discussed who then has to (a) make sure that only one person speaks at a time, (b) encourage everyone to voice their views and (c) sum up at the end of the meeting to check that everyone is sure about what has been decided.

The only item on today's agenda is the unusual number of office romances. This matter was raised by the Personnel Manager at the end of the last meeting when it was agreed to call in the Company's consultant psychologist, Professor A Smith, to find out what had been going on and why.

Professor Smith's report has been circulated to all six Managers. At present you are in your own office, alone, and have time to read the Report and perhaps make notes before sitting down with your colleagues.

Report: on the outbreak of non-platonic relationships among staff at the Head Office of Care Cosmetic Company

Facts I have confirmed an unduly high level of non-platonic relationships. In most cases, but not all, the initiators are females and span the age range. In general the males tend to take advantage of the opportunities offered. Each department is affected, and some relationships are interdepartmental.

Outcome Those affected, particularly the females, show lack of motivation in their work. In the words of one supervisor they 'cannot seem to keep their minds on the job'. When the relationships break up, usually after a few weeks, there is jealousy, ill-feeling and even deliberate sabotage of the work of colleagues. The situation is particularly sensitive because it involves some of the middle-aged and even one or two of the elderly.

Cause The problem began immediately after the offices were refurbished in three shades of brown – one for the furniture, another for the walls and the third for the carpets. One shade was chosen by the owner of Care Cosmetics and the other two were chosen by a sample poll of some of the staff. It is a well-known psychological fact that colour can affect human behaviour and, in this case, it appears that the chance combination of these particular shades of brown has had the effect of creating a short-term, powerful female-orientated aphrodisiac.

Treatment (1) The cause can be removed easily by either refurbishing walls, carpets or furniture or simply breaking up the dominant brown decor by putting pictures on the walls.

Treatment (2) The existing interpersonal tensions can be overcome by one of two options:

1 bringing in counselling specialists (I can recommend an excellent company)
2 doing nothing on the basis of 'Least said soonest mended' and letting time heal the wounds.

I recommend option 1, which would publicize the cause, help to remove feelings of guilt or shame and create a feeling of sympathy for those involved. A special issue of the Company's house journal could be devoted to the interpersonal problems and I would be prepared to contribute an article containing psychological advice.

Professor A Smith, Consultant Psychologist

---------- fold here ----------

Administration

---------- fold here ----------

Finance

---------- fold here ----------

Personnel

---------- fold here ----------

Production

---------- fold here ----------

Research

---------- fold here ----------

Sales

19 *Gene people*

Description

The Gene people is a simulation about Parano, a country with a minority race (the Qua) of above average intelligence. This situation has resulted in racial discrimination. The Qua make up 10 per cent of the population.

Objectives

To enhance the skills of communication, diplomacy, planning, presentation and team building in a racial context.

Time and numbers

The time will probably be one to three hours, depending on circumstances. The minimum number is seven (Ecology three, Justice two, Royal one, Television one). The maximum is limited only by the size of the space available. With more than about 15 participants, it may be a good idea to make 1 or 2 participants Organizers to help you out.

Resources

* Briefing sheet – one copy for each participant.
* International information sheet – one copy for each participant.
* Identification labels – one for each participant, using 'P' and 'Q' to identify race.
* A room with easily movable furniture.
* Scrap paper.

Method

1 Before the event begins, work out a good balance of jobs. For example, with 14 participants there could be 6 Ecology Party members of Parliament (all Parano), 4 Justice Party Members of Parliament (2 Parano and 2 Qua), 2 Royal personages (both Parano) and 2 Television journalists (1 Parano and 1 Qua). It is important that the Justice Party should be equally divided between Parano and Qua and if there are are two Television journalists at least one should be Qua.

2 Hand out the Briefing sheets – one copy to each participant. Hand out the International information sheets – one copy to each participant.

3 Allow the participants to pick their own (face down) Identification tags. Locate the Ecology, Justice, Royal and Television groups in the four corners of the room. Make scrap paper available.

4 Retrieve all copies of the Briefing sheets. Discuss the facilities, including the movement of furniture to accommodate a news conference (parliamentary debate, television news bulletin, party political broadcast, etc.).

5 Announce the time for the start of the debriefing.

Debriefing

The first stage could be to ask participants to take it in turns to explain any secret thoughts behind their strategies.

The debriefing can cover the extent to which participants were able to use and enhance their skills of communication and diplomacy. Did they consider various options? How well did they plan? Did they look for allies, make compromises, show initiatives? Were they sensitive to racial issues? Did the Royals distance themselves from the debate, or did they take sides? How well did the Justice Party Members of Parliament cope with their racial divide? Did the Ecology Party become anti-Qua? How effective were the presentations? Did anything surprising occur?

The Gene people is a simulation about Parano, a country with a minority race (the Qua) of above average intelligence. This situation has resulted in racial discrimination. The only way of telling the two races apart is that the native Parano have fair hair and the Qua have dark hair. The Qua make up 10 per cent of the population.

You are either:

* members of the Royal Family of the Kingdom of Parano, who are all native Parano
* Television journalists looking for news stories – at least one is Qua
* members of the majority party in Parliament, the governing Ecology Party, which has 60 seats – all are native Parano
* members of the minority Justice Party, which has 40 seats – half are native Parano and half are Qua.

The Identification labels of Members of Parliament and Television journalists will give their race – P = Parano, Q = Qua.

Details of the historical background to the situation are given in the extract from an International information sheet.

You can do whatever seems desirable so long as it is plausible, but if facilities are required you must consult the facilitator. Thus, you can, without consultation, elect a leader or draw up an advertisement or draft a bill, but if you wish to hold a parliamentary debate or give a news conference or a party political broadcast, then facilities and timing must be negotiated with the facilitator and possibly also with other participants.

Whenever an organized event is taking place, you must not ignore or disrupt it. For example, if you were in the middle of drafting a bill dealing with sex discrimination and the rival political party started giving a party political broadcast, you must stop, look, listen and behave with quiet respect. Not to do so in Parano is considered so disrespectful and insulting that it could easily cost you your job.

Do not playact. Do not insult people of a different race or pretend that you have been insulted by them. Behave professionally.

Developments in Parano

IN PARANO the ethnic majority (the Parano) make up 90 per cent of the population and the ethnic minority (the Qua) make up the remaining 10 per cent. However, the Qua have doubled in numbers over the past 20 years and this had led to racial tension and some outbreaks of violence, particularly over employment and housing.

Another cause of racial division is that the Qua have an average IQ of 120, compared with an average of 100 for native Parano, which has led to Qua people getting better jobs.

Qua people tend to keep themselves to themselves on a social level. On a professional and business level the two races usually get on well together and work harmoniously as a team.

The only physical difference between the two races is that the Parano all have fair hair whereas the Qua all have dark hair. Some years ago an international scientist put forward the theory that the higher than average Qua intelligence was due to a particular gene. As a result of this some Qua began proudly calling themselves 'the Gene people'. Recently, however, some Qua have complained that the phrase 'Gene people' has been used as a term of racial abuse by the native Parano.

The Qua people have always supported the Justice Party, mainly because this Party has always been keen to legislate on issues affecting race and equality. All Qua Members of Parliament belong to the Justice Party.

In the 100-member parliament, the Ecology Party have 60 seats – all are native Parano.

The Justice Party have 40 seats, equally split 20-20 between Parano and Qua. It is the first time that the Party has had the same number of Qua as Parano representatives in Parliament and the first time that the Qua have won 20 per cent of the seats. This means that the Qua, representing 10 per cent of the population, have double that percentage in Parliament.

The Royal Family, who are all Parano, chair parliamentary sessions but do not vote on bills. However, they have the power of veto. They can veto any bill once only so that, if it is re-introduced in identical terms after 12 months, the Royal veto would not apply.

Two recent court cases have caused (a) a demand from many Parano for a racial quota to be applied to top government jobs and top company jobs and (b) a demand from many Qua for new legislation to redefine racial abuse so that the offence depends on what the recipient of the remarks finds abusive rather than what most people think is abusive. The two cases are known as the Vee and Jay cases.

The Vee case involved the boss of a haulage company, Mr Vee, who restricted the number of Qua on his work-force to 10 per cent to match their proportion of the population. He did this reluctantly and only because of a strike threat by the local trade union, which had objected to Paranos losing their jobs to Quas. Mr Vee was accused under the Racial Equality Act of discriminating against Qua applicants by imposing the 10 per cent quota. He was found guilty on the grounds that employment should be given to those best qualified and not artificially restricted on grounds of race. He was fined. He appealed and lost.

The Jay case arose during the last election in which a defeated candidate, Miss Jay, a Qua, sued the winning candidate, a native Parano, for telling an election meeting 'We have far too many Gene people in top jobs and in Parliament and Miss Jay is one of the Gene people'. The Judge ruled that, although Miss Jay regarded the term 'Gene people' as racially offensive, both the Parano candidate and most of the people at the meeting regarded it purely as a descriptive term based on scientific evidence. Miss Jay lost her case. She took it to an appeals court and, again, lost.

Name:

Royal Family   (P)

Name:

Ecology Party   (P)

Name:

Justice Party   (P)

Name:

Justice Party   (Q)

Name:

Television journalist   (P)

Name:

Television journalist   (Q)

20 *Human zoo*

Description   This is a simulation set 20 years into the future in which rulers of Africa, America, Asia, Europe and the Middle East are faced with the problem of Space explorers who have arrived with the object of studying the main life form and requested a human zoo to enable them to do this without causing general disruption to life on Earth.

Objectives   To enhance the skills of diplomacy and planning in a context that involves race.

Time and numbers   The minimum number is five, in which case the event will last about an hour. Allow an hour and a half for larger numbers. With 20 or more participants, consider running the simulation as two (or more) parallel events.

Resources
* Briefing sheet – one copy for each participant.
* Working papers (five regions) – one for each team.
* Text of the message from the Space explorers – one copy for each team.
* Region identification tags – one for each team.
* Scrap paper.
* Furniture, arranged for separate meetings followed by a joint conference.

Method
1 Before you begin, it could be useful to mark the Briefing sheets with the names of the five regions and then place them marked side down so that when the participants pick their own sheets this will ensure a random distribution.

2 After the participants have read their Briefing sheets, divide them into groups and separate them as far apart as possible.

3 Indicate the time and location for the joint summit conference.

4 Retrieve the Briefing sheets and hand out the Region identification tags, the appropriate Working papers and the Text of the message from the Space explorers.

Debriefing   Start by asking each team in turn to reveal any secret strategies.

As a great deal was left to individual initiatives, it could be a good idea to discuss any unexpected occurrences or developments.

The main focus could be on the skills of diplomacy, planning and team building. Did the members of each team work well together? Did they find any personal prejudices getting in the way of presenting a case for their geographical region? To what extent were they diplomatic in their speech and their proposals? Were any verbal courtesies exchanged, such as 'honourable members', 'distinguished representatives'?

Were the Earthlings worried about the six weeks' deadline? Did they notice the unjustified assumption made by the advisers who referred to construction and building? The message itself used the word 'provide', which allows the option that the zoo could consist of an existing community plus some protective shields, observation panels and study areas and this may have been the intention of the Space explorers. If the Earthlings noticed 'provide' but still thought the project would take more than six weeks to complete, did they notice that the Space explorers used 'operational' rather than 'completion'? This would allow work to continue *after* the six weeks.

Did the Earthlings answer all four questions asked by the Space explorers and, if not, why not? Did they put any questions to the Space explorers – such as how long the study period would last? What would have been the likely reactions of the explorers to the decisions?

Did the Earthlings answer all four questions asked by the Space explorers and, if not, why not? Did they put any questions to the Space explorers – such as how long the study period would last? What would have been the likely reactions of the explorers to the decisions?

This is a simulation set in the future in which rulers of Africa, America, Asia, Europe and the Middle East are faced with the problem of Space explorers who have arrived with the object of studying the main life form and requested a human zoo to enable them to do this without causing general disruption to life on Earth.

You will first meet in your geographical groups. You will have the Text of the message from the Space explorers plus a Working paper drawn up by your own regional advisers. Then you come together for a joint summit conference.

Do not playact. Behave professionally.

Greetings Earthlings,

We are the crew of the spaceship Explorer. We study the main life forms of planets. We are here to study beings that are human.

We wish not to disrupt life on Earth. We, the Explorers, are radioactive and our physical appearance is highly repugnant to humans. We propose that you provide us with a human zoo. The zoo is not to exhibit different races, but to show different human behaviour in work and in play, in private life and in public life. We wish to study all typical human behaviour, except war.

The zoo must contain protective shields, observation panels and study areas. It must be at least six square miles in area. It must be operational within six weeks. Inhabitants of the zoo must not leave until we have completed our study.

We wish to know immediately:

* in which part of the world the zoo will be located
* who will inhabit it
* how the inhabitants will be chosen
* what behaviour will be included.

We should, with the greatest regret, consider any refusal or any delay as an hostile act and would, forthwith, order our Security arm to use whatever minimum force may be necessary to achieve our study objectives at a place of our own choosing and in a manner of our own choosing.

Africa: working paper

A key issue is whether we should propose that the zoo be constructed in Africa. If we made the offer, Africa could gain international gratitude, but some Africans will regard it as highly undesirable and will see it as a racial indignity.

The information requested by the Space explorers is not all that we should discuss. For example, Africa is not a wealthy continent and for us to pay for the construction, the upkeep and all the other expenses would be highly unfair, and probably impossible.

America: working paper

A key issue is whether we should propose that the zoo be constructed in America and, if so, in which part of America. If we made the offer, America could gain international gratitude, but some Americans will regard it as highly undesirable and see it as a great environmental danger.

The information requested by the Space explorers is not all that we should discuss. For example, the United States of America already pays more than its fair share of the world's debt and the costs for the building and upkeep of the zoo are likely to be very high indeed.

Asia: working paper

A key issue is whether we should propose that the zoo be constructed in Asia and, if so, in which country. If we made the offer, Asia could gain international gratitude, but some Asians will regard it as highly undesirable and will see it as a racial indignity and loss of face.

The information requested by the Space explorers is not all that we should discuss. For example, Asia is mainly made up of Third World countries that are not able to pay for the construction work, the upkeep and all the other expenses which would be involved.

Europe: working paper

A key issue is whether we should propose that the zoo be constructed in Europe and, if so, in which country. If we made the offer, Europe could gain international gratitude, but some Europeans will regard it as highly undesirable and will see it as a great ecological and environmental danger.

The information requested by the Space explorers is not all that we should discuss. For example, Europe already pays more than its fair share of the world's debt and the costs for the building of the zoo and its upkeep are likely to be very high indeed.

Middle East: working paper

A key issue is whether we should propose that the zoo be constructed in the Middle East and, if so, in which country. If we made the offer, the Middle East could gain international gratitude, but some of our people will see it as a great environmental danger and perhaps regard it as a racial indignity.

The information requested by the Space explorers is not all that we should discuss. For example, the Middle East already pays large sums to the international community and the costs for the building of the zoo and its upkeep are likely to be very high indeed.

Africa

America

Asia

Europe

Middle East

21 *Leaks*

Description

A simulation in which the Government of Alpha inquire into a serious leak of information to the media. The hidden agenda is that *all* the Ministers leaked the information independently.

Objectives

To enhance the skills of communication and diplomacy.

Time and numbers

About half an hour will be required for one group of four. With several groups, allow an hour so that comparisons of behaviour may be made in the debriefing. The minimum number is four and there is no maximum.

Resources

* Briefing sheet – one for each participant.
* Memo from the Prime Minister – one for each participant.
* Name tags – one for each of the four Ministers.
* Personal thoughts documents – one for each of the four Ministers.
* Scrap paper.

Method

1 Hand out the Briefing sheets – one for each participant.

2 Divide the participants at random into groups of four, separated as far apart as possible and preferably have each group seated around a table (if only to make it easier for each person to conceal their Personal thoughts document). If the total numbers do not divide equally by four, give the extra participants the role of Observers.

3 Place the Name tags face down and let the participants pick their own. Hand out the copies of the Memo from the Prime Minister – one to each participant.

4 Hand out the appropriate Personal thoughts documents, perhaps adding a warning that participants should now allow anyone else to see the document (which is not supposed to exist physically). It is, of course, vital that you hand the *right* Personal thoughts documents to the right Ministers. An alternative way of achieving confidentiality would be to ask the participants to stand, separate themselves and read their Personal thoughts documents for a few minutes (in their Ministerial offices) before arriving for the meeting.

5 Make the scrap paper available and retrieve the Briefing sheets.

Debriefing

The first step is to reveal the contents of the four Personal thoughts documents.

At the start of the simulation, everyone was guilty of the same breach of confidentiality, albeit for different reasons, but no one had actually told any lies. So one interesting point could be whether anyone lied at the meeting or simply went ahead and suggested ways of tightening security and/or devised some suitable statement for the media.

To what extent were the participants diplomatic and polite? Did they make personal accusations? Did they split up at any time to talk in pairs? How much of their Personal thoughts did they reveal? Would they have behaved differently if the event had been run a second time?

This is a simulation in which the Government of Alpha inquire into a serious leak of information to the press, radio and television.

You are one of four Ministers – Prime Minister, Minister of Defence, Minister of Finance and Minister of Internal Affairs.

You will have a Memo from the Prime Minister calling an urgent meeting of the inner cabinet, plus a Name tag and a few lines of Personal thoughts on how to deal with leaks of information.

Prime Minister's Office

MEMO

From: Prime Minister:

To: Ministers of Defence, Finance, Internal Affairs

I am calling an urgent meeting of the inner cabinet. As you must now be aware, a secret document has been leaked to the media. The document relates to the plan for cutting spending on the armed forces and increasing spending on the police. The wording of the reports show that it was a cabinet document of which only four copies existed – copies were held by myself and by the Ministers of Defence, Finance and Internal Affairs. The media say that the leak came from the inner cabinet and I can reach no other conclusion but that one of us leaked the document. We must strive to prevent such leaks occurring again. I hope you will all put forward suggestions.

Prime Minister

Minister of Defence

Minister of Internal Affairs

Minister of Finance

Prime Minister:
personal thoughts

I leaked the information because I want to undermine the Defence Minister who strongly opposes the plan for defence cuts. Public opinion will tend to support my own view, which favours the plan. Moreover, the Defence Minister will be suspected of leaking the document in order to gain support from Members of Parliament with military connections.

Minister of Defence:
personal thoughts

I leaked the information because I am strongly against the proposed cuts in the armed forces and I can count on support from Members of Parliament with military connections.

However, the Minister of Internal Affairs could come under suspicion of leaking the document in order to gain popularity among the middle-class voters, who are in favour of strengthening law and order.

Minister of Internal Affairs:
personal thoughts

I leaked the information in order to gain support from middle-class voters, who are in favour of strengthening law and order.

However, the Finance Minister could come under suspicion because an increase in spending on law and order means that no money would be available for tax cuts and tax cuts would virtually guarantee that the Finance Minister would be seen as the most likely successor to the Prime Minister.

Minister of Finance:
personal thoughts

I leaked the information because an increase in spending on law and order means that no money would be available for tax cuts and tax cuts would virtually guarantee that I would be seen as the most likely successor to the Prime Minister.

However, it is possible to suspect that the Prime Minister leaked the information in order to gain public support for the plan and undermine the position of the Defence Minister who opposes cutting defence spending.

22 *Romantic dream*

Description

This is a simulation of an author's dream in which the participants are six Occupations in search of their gender and their position in a romantic novel in which the main character must be a female but must not be the secretary. Because the author cannot deal with more than two people at a time in the dream, the characters have to meet in pairs. It can be run in the format of an icebreaker.

Objectives

To enhance the skills of communication, planning and team building.

Time and numbers

If there are six participants, the event should last about half an hour. With more than six, the event will take about an hour. With 12 or more participants, consider the possibility of running the simulation as separate parallel events.

Resources

* Briefing sheet – one for each participant.
* Six Occupation tags – one tag for each participant.
* Dream form – one for each participant.
* Scrap paper.

Method

1 Before introducing the event, make sure that you have the right number and distribution of job Occupations – to have two police officers but no secretary would be a disaster.

2 Hand out the Briefing sheets and set a deadline for the start of the debriefing.

3 If there are more than six participants, specify that if two people meet and find they have the same Occupation tag, they must merge into the same Occupation and stick together.

4 If your main aim is to run it as an icebreaker, it might be a good idea to fix a time for meetings and give a signal for them to change partners. If your aim is mainly to enhance the skills of communication, planning and team building, you need set no time limit for meetings, but perhaps ask participants to end their talk fairly quickly if someone is waiting to meet them.

5 Hand out copies of the Occupation tags and the Dream forms – one of each to each participant. Make the scrap paper available. Retrieve the Briefing sheets.

Debriefing

If the simulation was run as several events in parallel, it may be useful to start with each dream team having a mini-debriefing to work out what was proposed and decided and also what difficulties there were in achieving a memorable dream. They can then report back to a joint session. If there was only one dream, it could still be a good idea for the participants to have a mini-debriefing to work out what happened.

A key issue is likely to be the ways in which the participants tried to overcome the difficulty of having to meet in pairs. Did they make anyone a coordinator? Did each person try to become the female lead character? Was planning discussed or did they talk only about a plot and characterization? Did anyone make a list of options? Were there any disputes involving gender? How friendly and cooperative were the participants? Did anyone come up with bright ideas?

This is a simulation of an author's dream in which you represent the Occupations of six characters in an unwritten romantic novel.

The author had a meeting yesterday with the publisher and explained that there would be six Occupations for the main characters – secretary, boss, trade union official, sales manager, boss of a rival company and police officer. The author proposed that the central character should be the secretary who would be a woman. The publisher replied that this would have been fine for the last novel, but now the policy was to get away from sex stereotypes. The publisher accepted that the central character should be a woman, but said she must not be the secretary.

The author is now having a dream and you are one of the Occupations of the six main characters. You must try to reach agreement on three points:

1 the Occupation of the leading character, who must be female
2 the gender of the people in the other jobs
3 a rough outline of the plot.

As it is a dream, the author has no control over you, but the author cannot hold in mind more than two Occupations at a time. Therefore, you must meet in pairs only – never in threes or more.

The more you agree, the more likely the author will be able to remember the dream, in which case you could gain useful employment as a plot idea.

You will receive an Occupation tag plus a Dream form to record who you met and what was proposed. You can meet the same participant twice, but preferably not until you have met everyone else.

Secretary

Boss

Trade union official

Sales manager

Boss of a rival company

Police officer

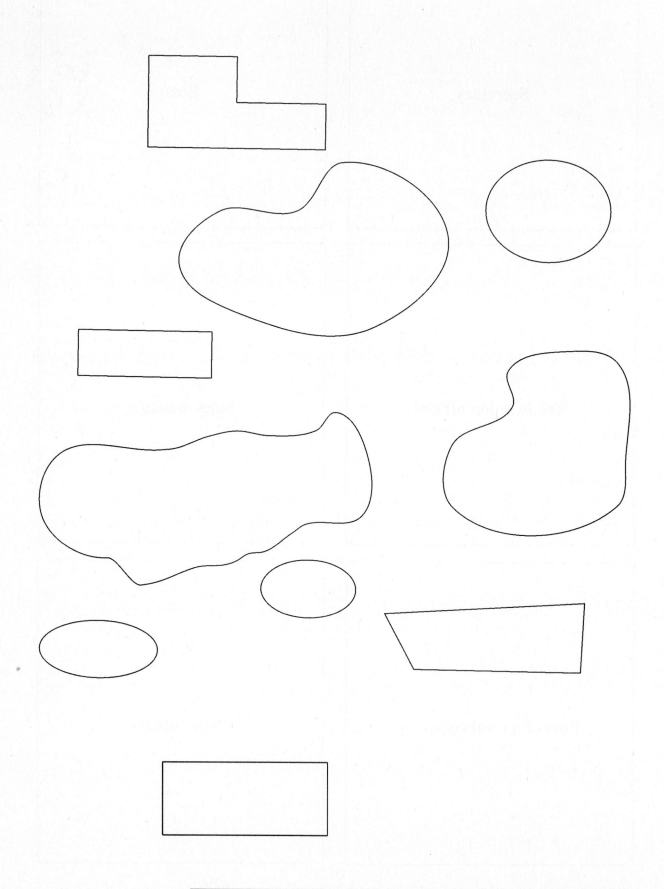

23 *Sorcerer's apprentice*

Description
This is a simulation of interviews by Sorcerers or Sorceresses seeking Apprentices. The simulation can be run in the format of an icebreaker.

Objectives
To enhance the skills of negotiation and team building.

Time and numbers
It will probably last between half an hour and an hour. It could work with a minimum of four participants. There is no maximum number. With 20 or more participants, allow up to an hour and a half because more time will be required in the debriefing for explanations, comparisons and comments.

Resources
* Briefing sheet – one for each participant.
* Magic sheet – one for each participant, with spare copies made available.

Method
1 If your main concern is to run the event as an icebreaker with people meeting as many other people as reasonably possible, it could be a good idea to fix a time limit for each meeting and give a signal for participants to change partners. If your main objective is enhancing the skills of negotiation and team building, the meetings can be longer and more flexible in their timing.

2 Arrange for sufficient space so that meetings in pairs can be well spaced out and reasonably private. Hand out the Briefing sheets and the Magic sheets – one of each to each participant.

3 Announce details of the timing arrangements. It could be a good idea to allocate a space where people could go after their meetings break up so that they can readily see who is available for interview. Retrieve the Briefing sheets.

Debriefing
The first step could be to collect information about any interesting developments that occurred in the interviews.

How much imagination and plausible additions were shown during the interviews? Did anyone give the impression of being a real Sorcerer or Sorceress on a professional level or a real Apprentice on a professional level? Were participants business-like, mystical or personally emotive? Were people polite and helpful? How effective were the skills of negotiation and team building? Did any gender issues arise? Did any ethical issues (right and wrong, good and bad, truth and falsehood) arise? Did the participants prefer the role of employer or the applicant for the job?

This is a simulation of interviews by Sorcerers or Sorceresses seeking Apprentices. Everyone meets in pairs and changes role halfway through each meeting. When you meet someone, decide who will have which role first. The event takes place on the evening of the seventh silver phase of the moon to find the best magical flux. As it is an evening of flux, no decisions can be taken until the morrow, so no Apprentices are signed up during the event.

Before you start, you might like to decide whether you are interested in pursuing general purpose sorcery or whether you are interested in a special type of magic, say, cauldron magic.

If you are a Sorceress you can assume that you have the same powers, the same prestige, the same scale of fees and the same awesomeness as your male colleagues. Similarly, aspiring female Apprentices can be assumed to have equal rights, equal respect, equal powers, equal pay and equal opportunities.

The Magic sheet is for you to record your magical contacts and magical thoughts. How you use the signs on the sheet is up to you.

Real name: _____

Magic name: _____

24 *To the courts*

Description

This is a simulation about a civil claim for damages by a home owner whose fence has been damaged by a Car owner. Both sides have Legal advisers and have the choice of an out-of-court settlement or a court action in which they can be represented by either a top, expensive lawyer or an average, less expensive lawyer.

Objectives

To enhance the skills of negotiation, problem solving and time management.

Time and numbers

The time required will depend on whether the case is rerun and how many participants are involved. Each group could rerun the case several times by changing functions and partners. Another way to rerun the case is for several groups to split up.

The minimum number of participants is four and there is no maximum. With four and without a rerun, the event should take about half an hour. If there are 20 participants and no rerun, the event will probably last about an hour because of the time taken in the debriefing to explain, compare and comment on what happened in the different groups. With several groups and several reruns, the event could take up to two hours.

Resources

* Briefing sheet – one copy for each participant.
* Facts of the case – one copy for each participant.
* Schedule of legal costs – one copy for each participant.
* Identification tags – four for each group.
* Sufficient space for private meetings between client and legal adviser.
* Scrap paper.

Method

1 Hand out the Briefing sheets – one copy for each participant. If there are eight or more participants, you could mark the Briefing sheets so as to divide the participants into groups of four. Place the sheets face down and let the participants pick their own. If there are participants left over, they could be Colleagues of the legal advisers or Friends of the clients.

2 Discuss the questions of reruns, time limits, space for private conversations and so on.

3 Hand out the Identification tags at random, perhaps placing them face down.

4 Hand out the Facts of the case and the Schedule of legal costs – one of each for each participant. Ask the participants to separate (not four of them sitting round the same table) so that they can read the documents individually. Give them time to work out the costs of various options before the meetings in pairs between client and Legal adviser.

5 Make scrap paper available. Retrieve the Briefing sheets.

Debriefing

The debriefing could begin by asking whether the participants had worked out the various options. For example, an out-of-court settlement would depend on the time taken to negotiate an agreement whereas the compensation awarded by the court depends on whether the clients choose top lawyers or average lawyers.

Clients	Lawyers	Fee	Judgement	Result
Fence owner	Top	4	5	1
Car owner	Top	4	5	-9
Fence owner	Average	2	5	3
Car owner	Average	2	5	-7
Fence owner	Top	4	7	3
Car owner	Average	2	7	-9
Fence owner	Average	2	3	1
Car owner	Top	4	3	-7

This means that there is an even chance for the Fence owner to gain one litig (currency used in this event) or three litigs. There is an even chance for the Car owner to lose seven or nine litigs, If, however, an out-of-court settlement of five litigs was agreed within 60 seconds, the Fence owner would gain four litigs and the Car owner lose six litigs, both clients ending up one litig more favourable than the best possible court case result and three litigs more favourable than the worst possible court case result.

The debriefing could also look at whether Legal advisers and clients built up good working relationships. Did they pass on their conclusions about the win/ lose court options? Legal advisers who sought to make as much money out of their clients as possible might not have acted in the law firm's best interests if the client was dissatisfied.

This is a simulation about a civil claim for damages by a home owner whose fence has been damaged by a Car owner. Both sides have Legal advisers and have the choice of an out-of-court settlement or a court action in which they can be represented by either a top, expensive lawyer or an average, less expensive lawyer.

You will be in one of four roles: Fence owner, fence owner's Legal adviser, Car owner, car owner's Legal adviser.

The first stage is for you to read the documents individually, separately, and perhaps work out the financial consequences of the options. The second stage consists of two separate meetings between individual clients and their own Legal advisers. These meetings can last for up to five minutes without a fee being charged. Subsequent meetings can be arranged as desired, except that the two clients can never meet without their Legal advisers being present.

It is in your own interests to keep a careful check of the time (and therefore the cost) of meetings.

The currency in this simulation is the litig.

Facts of the case

The case is a civil claim for compensation. The undisputed facts are that the Car owner knocked down the garden fence and that the Fence owner was sitting nearby but was not hurt. The Car owner's insurance covered the cost of repairing both the fence and the car, but the Fence owner is claiming damages for non-insurable items, namely for shock and distress caused by the event.

Compensation awarded by the court will vary as follows:

* if both are top lawyers or both average lawyers – 5 litigs compensation
* if Fence owner has a top lawyer and Car owner an average lawyer – 7 litigs compensation
* if Car owner has a top lawyer and Fence owner an average lawyer – 3 litigs compensation.

Either client can request their Legal adviser to ask for a conference with the other party to discuss an out-of-court settlement. The bargaining at such a conference is between the two clients. The Legal advisers must keep silent, but each can be asked questions by their own client, in which case they must reply quickly using one of two words – 'Yes' or 'No' – so the questions should be framed accordingly.

Either client can break off the conference at any time. An agreement is concluded only after both clients have said the word 'Agreed'.

Schedule of legal costs

The costs are as follows:

* Legal advisers make no charge to their client for a preliminary five-minute discussion about (a) whether to try for an out-of-court settlement and (b), if the choice is to go before the court, whether to employ a top lawyer or an average lawyer as counsel

* any further discussion costs one litig for each five minutes or part thereof, except in the case of a discussion between client and Legal adviser held as a result of the other party requesting a conference to discuss an out-of-court settlement

* any client proposing a conference to discuss an out-of-court settlement must pay one litig in advance to their Legal adviser, which is not refunded if the other party does not agree to attend such a conference

* if a conference is held, each client pays their Legal adviser an attendance fee of one litig for each minute or part thereof, the first minute being free to the client who paid the one litig advance fee

* going to court with a top lawyer is four litigs

* going to court with an average lawyer is two litigs.

Fence owner

Car owner

Legal adviser to fence owner

Legal adviser to car owner

Creativity areas

25 *Creating portraits*

Description This is a simulation in which Artists and Patrons create portraits in a step-by-step manner, changing roles halfway through each meeting. It can be run in the format of an icebreaker.

Objectives To enhance the skills of communication and diplomacy.

Time and numbers Depending on numbers and your objectives, the event could last between an hour and an hour and a half. The greater the number of participants, the more time would be required in the debriefing for explanations, descriptions, comparisons and comments. Probably the minimum number is four. There is no maximum.

Resources
* Briefing sheet – one copy for each participant.
* Artist's sheet – one copy for each participant.
* Patron's sheet – one copy for each participant.
* Questions sheet – one copy for the facilitator.

Method

1 The event involves the answering of ten questions, one at a time, privately, in pairs of Artist and Patron. Participants switch roles halfway through each meeting and each participant has the job of devising a portrait of two people. You should conceal the questions so that participants do not know where the questions are leading, thus making it easier for them to build up a portrait gradually by discussion rather than looking at the final questions and working towards preconceived ideas.

2 Divide the total negotiating time by ten and set that as the time limit for dealing with each question, perhaps allowing a few minutes buffer time in case the meetings take longer than you expect. With 11 participants, everyone would meet everyone else. With only three or four participants, everyone would meet the same person two or three times. With 20 or more participants, you could consider running two events in parallel. Discuss the timing and locations, trying to allow enough space for pairs to meet privately. If you wish to shorten the event, you could merge the questions into five pairs – one and two, three and four, etc.

3 Hand out the Briefing sheets, the Artist's sheets and the Patron's sheets – one of each to each participant.

4 Allow the participants time to fill in the answers to the two preliminary questions on the Artist's sheets.

5 Retrieve the Briefing sheets.

6 Divide the participants at random into pairs and announce the first question (or first pair of questions) to the whole group.

7 Halfway through the meeting it could be useful to remind them to change roles as some pairs might become so interested in one Artist's portrait that they do not allow enough time to discuss the portrait of the other Artist.

8 At the end of the time period ask the participants to record the meeting briefly on both sheets and change partners. Announce the next question.

Debriefing

The first step could be for Artists to give a brief description of their paintings – without any discussion. The descriptions could include any unusual (interesting, important, significant) episode in the creative process.

In the joint discussion the key questions are likely to focus on the skills of communication and diplomacy. Communication between Artists and Patrons are sometimes acrimonious – was there any acrimony during the event? How many answers (if any) were marked 'D' for disagreement? Were Patrons diplomatic? Were Artists polite? Did Patrons find that they were trying to impose the same ideas on each Artist they met? Despite the request in the Briefing sheet for Artists to keep an open mind during discussions, did they find themselves working towards their own preconceived ideas of what the finished painting should look like? How imaginative were both Artists and Patrons? How flexible were they in accommodating new ideas that might have interfered with any preconceptions? Which role did most participants prefer – Artist or Patron? Why?

How different, if at all, were the answers to questions nine and ten compared with questions seven and eight?

How well did the event work as an icebreaker? Were contacts superficial or profound, perfunctory or friendly, dull or stimulating? Did anything unusual occur?

This is a simulation in which Artists and Patrons create portraits in a step-by-step manner, changing roles halfway through each meeting. Concentrate on portraiture and do not invent details about yourself. All the Artists are competent, all the Patrons are wealthy and none have international reputations.

There is one question to answer at each of ten meetings and the questions will be announced by the facilitator at the start of each meeting. Do not meet anyone twice unless you have already met everyone else.

You will receive an Artist's sheet for describing the portrait and a Patron's sheet for recording anything that occurred which particularly interested the Patron.

The Artist's sheet starts with two preliminary questions that you must answer (privately and individually) before you meet anyone. The next ten spaces are for you to record the development of your portrait during ten meetings. Restrict each answer to the particular question and do not give additional information, otherwise you may find you have answered a question that will be asked later.

Do not try to envisage your portrait from the start – keep your mind as blank as the canvas and negotiate the portrait bit by bit. If there is disagreement, the Artist's view prevails but the letter 'D' for disagreement must be written after the answer.

The Patron's sheet also has ten numbers for the ten meetings. It is for you to record the names of the Artists you meet plus any comments. If nothing noteworthy occurred, then leave the Comments section blank.

You do not have to reveal what you have written on your Patron's sheet, but you do have to reveal your Artist's sheet at each meeting.

Artist's sheet

Name: _____

The year is? _____ (any year after about 1600, but not set in the future)

The country in which you have your studio is?
(any country with a tradition of portrait painting) _____

Questions	Patrons	Answers
1		
2		
3		
4		
5		
6		
7		
8		
9		
10		

Patron's sheet

Name: _____

Questions	Artists	Comments
1		
2		
3		
4		
5		
6		
7		
8		
9		
10		

Questions sheet

1 What is the background? (Roman ruins, sea, Victorian drawing room, etc.)

2 What is in the foreground, apart from the two people. (Desk, tree, wineglass, laptop computer, etc.)

3 What does the person on the left look like? (Sex, age, race, beauty, clothing, etc.)

4 What does the person on the right look like? (Sex, age, race, beauty, clothing, etc.)

5 What is the person on the left doing? (Standing, holding something, smiling, etc.)

6 What is the person on the right doing? (Standing, holding something, smiling, etc.)

7 What do you think the person on the left thinks and feels?

8 What do you think the person on the right thinks and feels?

9 There is no Artist, no canvas, no painting, no viewing public — just two real people side by side in the situation you have negotiated. You are the person on the left. What do you think and feel?

10 There is no Artist, no canvas, no painting, no viewing public — just two real people side by side in the situation you have negotiated. You are the person on the right. What do you think and feel?

26 *Empty boxes lecture*

Description   This is a simulation in which College staff have to prepare and deliver a brief lecture on counselling, having only the Diagram of empty boxes and arrows produced by the lecturer who was to take the class but is ill.

Objectives   To enhance the skills of planning, presentation and team building.

Time and numbers   With a small number of participants, the event would probably last about half an hour to an hour. The minimum number is four, allowing for two teams of two. There is no maximum number, but the greater the numbers, the more time should be allowed for the additional presentations.

Resources
* Briefing sheet – one for each participant.
* Memo – one for each group.
* Diagram – one for each group.
* Scrap paper and perhaps large sheets of paper, overhead projector, etc.

Method   1 Depending on numbers, the random distribution of groups can be achieved by marking the Briefing sheets and allowing the participants to pick their own. Each group should consist of at least two participants to ensure an interchange of ideas, but do not have more than four in a group otherwise some people might be marginalized when it comes to the presentation.

2 Explain the facilities available for the lecture (table, flip chart, overhead projector, etc.) and announce the minimum and maximum time for each lecture. Decide and announce whether the audience will be allowed to ask questions after each lecture.

3 Announce the location of the lectures. It is preferable to have a separate area for the lectures and have participants standing up, rather than sitting at their own tables. In order to achieve a reasonable degree of realism, the chairs should be arranged so that the audience looks like an audience, not like diners in a restaurant.

4 Divide and separate the groups.

5 Retrieve all the Briefing sheets and hand out the Memo and Diagram – one of each to each group, plus scrap paper and any other facilities. Keep some Diagrams handy as spares.

6 Run the lectures.

Debriefing   Depending on numbers, it might be a good idea for each group to debrief themselves. As the presentations will have been public, the groups could look at the process rather than the result, including ideas that were not considered or ideas that were considered and rejected, especially in the light of their actual knowledge of counselling.

The joint debriefing will probably concentrate on skills of planning, presentation and team building. How difficult was it to plan a plausible lecture within the confines of the empty Diagram? Was there a search for options or was the first plausible idea seized upon and developed? Did individuals start by picking up their pens and working on their own or was there discussion about the best way to proceed?

Did the quality and plausibility of the presentations depend upon a group's knowledge of counselling? If a group knew nothing about counselling, was it able to invent plausible and perhaps even effective and appropriate jargon? Did lack of actual knowledge mean that the individual presenters were hesitant, defensive and unconvincing?

Did each team work as a team both in the planning and in the presentation? If the presentation was shared equally, was it also shared plausibly? ('At this stage, at the interaction of these two boxes, I want to hand over to my colleague, X, who has contributed a good deal to the study of this area of interlocking constructs.')

Briefing   26 Empty boxes lecture

This is a simulation in which College staff have to prepare and deliver a brief lecture on counselling, having only the Diagram of empty boxes and arrows produced by the lecturer who was to take the class but is ill.

You work in groups and will have a Memo from the Dean of the College plus the Diagram to be used with your lecture. The lecture itself should be a team effort, with each member participating in some way.

Affersedge College

From: Dean

To: English Faculty Study Group

Would you please deliver a brief lecture on counselling to the new intake of students who have opted for this course. The lecturer has been taken ill and is able to provide only an empty flow chart. No other expert on the subject is available. As you are from the English Department I feel sure that you can improvize perfectly adequately – just fill in the boxes with some counselling-type words. If you cannot think of any, then use 'input', 'output' and 'feedback', but I feel sure you can do better than that.

In your lecture, simply explain your diagram – 'This leads to this', that sort of thing. You do not have to talk about what your labels mean unless you want to and you should concentrate on the interaction of the boxes and arrows. Anyway, it always sounds more impressive if you stick to talking about labels and generalizations and aims rather than talking about real people and real examples. Less danger that way.

By the way, how about about using the word 'construct' rather than 'concept'? It is the sort of word that can nudge the listeners off balance as they will probably be unsure if it means 'concept'. Because 'construct' can also mean 'to build' it has a nice degree of ambiguity that sounds as if you know what you are talking about. The listeners will probably be happy to accept your word as an expert rather than try to work out what it all means. Anyway, that is just a thought. You will probably come up with some useful and impressive ambiguities.

Think of another, impressive way of saying 'Counselling is a good thing'. The important thing is not to make any jokes. Show them you are really serious. Only serious people are plausible.

I am sure that in the knowledge of the impending cuts in College staff you will be able to confirm your versatility and indispensability.

Diagram

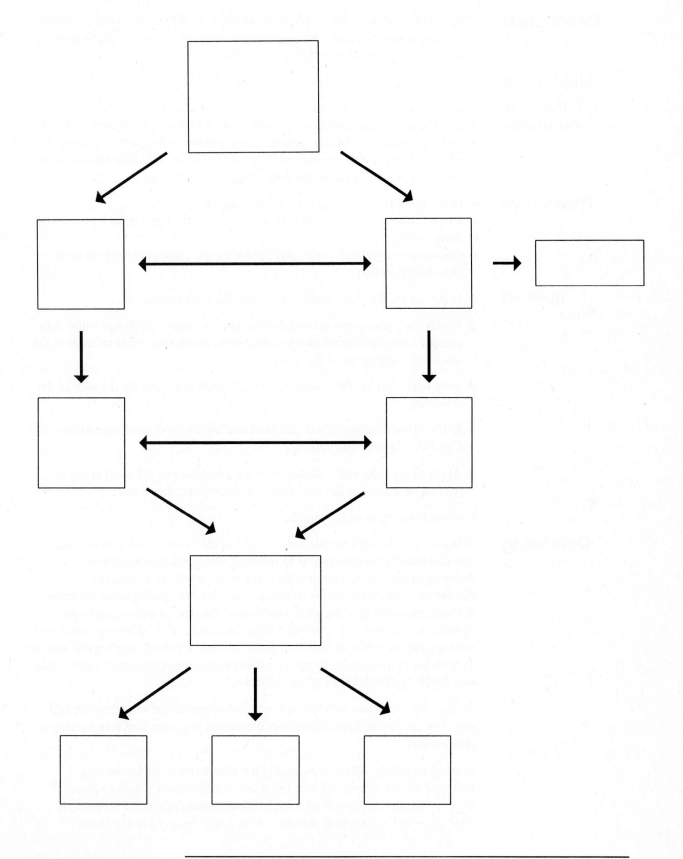

27 *Ghost stories*

Description   This is a simulation in which participants begin as eighteenth-century Writers describing a ghost and later become modern hotel Managers trying to make use of the ghost story for publicity purposes.

Objectives   To enhance the skills of communication and planning.

Time and numbers   With a small number of participants, the event would probably last about an hour. The minimum number is four, allowing for two teams of two. There is no maximum number, but the greater the number of participants, the more time should be allowed because of the need to explain, compare and comment on different groups' work in the debriefing.

Resources
*   Briefing sheet – one copy for each participant.
*   Extract from *Good Hotels in Country Areas* – one copy for each participant.
*   Scrap paper.
*   Self-assessment sheet – one copy for each participant (see suggestions in **Debriefing** section).

Method
1   Hand out the Briefing sheets – one copy for each participant.

2   Divide the participants at random into pairs or threes. With more than four groups, it may be a good idea to locate them around the walls to assist in the clockwise passing on of the stories.

3   Set a time limit for the completion of the ghost story and for the start of the debriefing.

4   Retrieve the Briefing sheets and hand out the copies of the Extract from *Good Hotels in Country Areas*.

5   At the time set for the completion of the ghost stories, ask each group to pass on their story to the next group in a clockwise direction.

6   Make the scrap paper available.

Debriefing   This is one of the Five simple events listed in the Introduction and the easiest way to debrief a simple event is to ask the participants to fill in the Self-assessment sheets individually and use the results as a basis for discussion. The alternative is to take a more flexible approach and tailor the debriefing according to the particular course, the type of participants and significant episodes that occurred during the action. The following questions and suggestions could be used as a guide not only for the debriefing but also as a check-list of the sorts of things you could watch for in the action itself. (See also **Running the debriefing**, Introduction.)

Arrange for some way in which groups can communicate what they did and why they did it – perhaps debriefing themselves in groups and then making a presentation.

In communicating the ghost story, did the Writers try to make the text authentic – for example did they use a few old-fashioned words or phrases? Was the writing in the style of a modern business memo or did it convey a sense of period and suggest that the Writer really believed in the ghost?

Was any use made of the location – tower, mill, pond, village green, tennis courts or croquet lawn?

In writing the publicity leaflet, how did the teams cope with the problem of trying to attract people without frightening them off? Did they simply summarize the story or did they add some observations or comments of their own? Did they invent any recent sightings of the ghost (see last sentence of Briefing sheet) and, if so, how did they justify the untruth?

This is a simulation in which you begin as an eighteenth-century Writer describing (and believing in) a ghost. You later become a modern hotel Manager trying to make use of the ghost story for publicity purposes.

In the first stage you will receive an Extract from *Good Hotels in Country Areas* dealing with Manor Born Hotel, formerly the Manor House, that gives some details about the location. You then project yourself back in time and become eighteenth-century Writers and produce a short ghost story as a joint effort. It must be about a ghost at the Manor House. Relate local gossip. Say that, although you have not personally seen the ghost, you have been told such and such. If you do not complete the story by the deadline, then write half a word and draw a wobbly line downwards to indicate that something nasty has happened to prevent the story being completed.

Pass on your ghost story to the next group in a clockwise direction. You are now Managers of the Manor Born Hotel, having just discovered the eighteenth-century manuscript passed to you. Your job is to write a one-page advertisement for the Hotel that refers to the alleged ghost. However, you have no personal knowledge that anyone in recent times has ever claimed to have seen the ghost.

Extract from:

Good Hotels in Country Areas

Manor Born Hotel

The hotel is a renovated eighteenth-century manor house. The historical structure – wooden beams, low-ceilinged bedrooms – has been kept intact. There are 23 bedrooms, each with a bathroom. The hotel has a small but elegant lounge, a spacious dining room and two bars. The Tower, which is part of the Manor House, contains three suites. The grounds include tennis courts and a croquet lawn. On one side of the hotel are the ruins of a seventeenth-century corn mill and on the other side is a picturesque village green with a large pond.

How did you begin? For example, did you have a brainstorming session? Did you look at various options?

Did your ghost story reveal
* who the Writer was – vicar, Lord of the Manor, school teacher?
* the context – letter to a friend, entry in a diary, part of a book?
* whether the writer believed in the ghost?

Did the story use any of the locations – the tower, the mill, the pond, the tennis courts or the village green?

Did your ghost story read like an article in today's newspaper or like something written hundreds of years ago?

In the advertisement for the hotel did you consider the possibility of people being frightened away by mention of a ghost and, if so, how did you deal with this aspect?

How do you assess yourself?

Skills	Poor	Fair	Good	Excellent
Creativity				
Communication				
Planning				
(Other)				

How do you assess your team?

Skills	Poor	Fair	Good	Excellent
Creativity				
Communication				
Planning				
(Other)				

28 *Hyp-hen*

Description This is a simulation of a group test for Applicants for the job of creative writers to Media Comedy Enterprises. They have to insert a hyphen in words and redefine the meanings accordingly.

Objectives To enhance the skills of communication, presentation and team building.

Time and numbers The time required is about half an hour for small numbers and more than an hour for large numbers. The minimum number is four (two pairs). There is no maximum.

Resources
* Briefing sheet – one copy for each participant.
* Group test instructions – one for each group.
* Hyp-hen form – one for each group (plus some spare copies).
* Scrap paper, and perhaps larger sheets, overhead projector, etc.

Method
1 Hand out the Briefing sheets – one copy for each participant. If you have more than about ten participants it could be a good idea to have a pair representing Media Comedy Enterprises for the purpose of arranging the timing and order of the presentations.

2 Announce the location of the presentations.

3 Divide the participants at random into groups and separate the groups.

4 Retrieve all the Briefing sheets and hand out the Group test instructions and the Hyp-hen form.

Debriefing Depending on the numbers it might be a good idea for each group to debrief themselves. This can be followed by a meeting of all groups, the meeting beginning with a brief account from each group of what ideas were accepted and rejected.

Apart from discussing the humour (subtlety, incongruity, wit) of the items, the debriefing will probably concentrate on the planning, presentations and team building. Was there a search for options or was the first plausible idea seized upon and developed? Did individuals start by picking up their pens and working on their own or was there any discussion about the best way to proceed? Did the quality of the memos depend more on good teamwork or on bright individuals?

Did the participants spend so much time on the memo that they left the presentation to the last minute, with team members looking at each other and not sure who would say what? Was the presentation run by one person or was it a team effort? Did any team make use of charts, notices or graphics?

If there was a team representing Media Comedy Enterprises, did they take charge of the organization or sit back and hope that the event would organize itself? Did they give clear guidance on the timing, the facilities available and the order of the presentations? Did they behave with authority or did they hide? What did the team think of the Applicants and vice versa?

This is a simulation of a group test for Applicants for the job of creative writers to Media Comedy Enterprises, who have to insert a hyphen in words and redefine the meanings accordingly.

You will receive a copy of Group test instructions from Media Comedy Enterprises plus the Hyp-hen form for you to fill in. You will have scrap paper.

Media Comedy Enterprises

Group test instructions

In one sentence write a busi-ness me-mo us-ing the hyp-hen in bro-ken langu-age and de-fine your words.

For example, in the above sentence the definitions might be:

* busi-ness   the ability to appear busy
* me-mo   a document designed to enhance the prestige of 'me' – the sender
* us-ing   in-group behaviour, as in 'us'
* hyp-hen   over-enthusiastic marketing of chicken products
* bro-ken   relative knowledge or know-how (lit: the brother of knowing)
* langu-age   old-fashioned usage or boring, soporific usage
* de-fine   to make cloudy, unclear, confused.

Hyp-hen form

Group names: _____

Sentence:

_____

_____

_____

_____

Definitions:

_____

_____

_____

_____

_____

_____

_____

_____

_____

_____

29 *Levitation pill*

Description   This is a simulation to prepare a secret report for the Government of Alpha on the possible consequences of releasing the levitation pill.

Objectives   To enhance the skills of planning and team building.

Time and numbers   The time required is up to an hour for small numbers and more than an hour for large numbers. The minimum number is four and there is no maximum.

Resources
* Briefing sheet – one copy for each participant.
* Ministry tags – a set of four for each group.
* Memo from the Prime Minister – one for each participant.
* Secret report – one for each participant,
* Library information – one for each participant.
* Recommendations form – one for each group (with spares available).
* Scrap paper.

Method

1 Hand out the Briefing sheets – one copy for each participant.

2 Divide the participants at random into groups of four and separate the groups. If the numbers will not divide equally, then have one or two people sharing roles.

3 Retrieve all the Briefing sheets and hand out the Ministry tags at random, perhaps placing them face down and allowing participants to pick their own.

4 Hand out the copies of the Memo from the Prime Minister, the Secret report and the Library information – one of each to each participant. It is useful to allow the participants time to read this information on their own (as if in their own separate offices) and to think themselves into the roles before the meeting begins.

5 Hand out the Recommendations forms – one to each group – and set a deadline for the completion of the recommendations. Make scrap paper available.

Debriefing   Depending on the numbers, it might be a good idea for each group to debrief themselves. A meeting of all the groups can then begin with a brief account from each group of what ideas and plans they accepted and rejected.

In the subsequent discussion, the emphasis will probably be more on the process than the result. For example, did they have a brainstorming session? Did they search for options and ideas or did they set to work on the first plausible idea that came up? Did they divide the work up, perhaps each person searching for ideas related to their ministerial duties?

Did anyone take the chair or suggest an agenda or summarize what was being discussed and decided? Although a joint report was required, did anyone forget that they worked for a specific Ministry and ignore the implications of the pill for that Ministry?

This is a simulation to prepare a secret report to the Prime Minister of Alpha on the implications of the levitation pill.

You are a group of four senior staff from the Ministry of Defence, the Ministry of Home Affairs, the Ministry of the Environment and the Ministry of Industry and Agriculture. The Committee was set up by the Prime Minister and reports directly to the Prime Minister. It is a secret Committee that comes under Alpha's Defence of the Realm Act.

You will each have a Memo from the Prime Minister, a Secret report and Library information. The group will have a Recommendations form.

----------- fold here -----------

Defence

----------- fold here -----------

Home Affairs

----------- fold here -----------

Environment

----------- fold here -----------

Industry and Agriculture

Residence of the Prime Minister

From: Prime Minister
To: Committee

Please produce immediate recommendations regarding the implications of the levitation pill. Apart from myself only the research staff at Alphamoor know about the levitation pill, apart from a brief and misleading reference in the *Alpha Times* obituary of Miss Lal. One point you must deal with is whether this secrecy should be maintained.

Find enclosed:

1 the report from Alphamoor
2 Library information.

Alphamoor Research Station

From: Chief Research Officer
To: Prime Minister

Following your instruction, I personally was in charge of the experiment and kept all information on a need-to-know basis.

A total of 50 levitation pills were used during the experiment, half of which had been produced by Miss Lal before her death and the other half of which were manufactured by our Chief Research Chemist, based on analysis of the ingredients of Miss Lal's pills. The unit cost of a pill was about £20, but this could be reduced considerably if manufactured in quantity.

Ten members of staff participated in the experiment. Each took one pill a day and the experiment lasted for five days. No alcohol, smoking or other drugs were allowed, not even tea or coffee. All floats and flights were under the direction of myself.

Eight of the ten subjects levitated successfully. By the fifth day they were able to achieve forward flight at speeds of up to 10 miles an hour and for distances of up to one mile and for altitudes of up to 10 feet. The two subjects who failed to levitate (one male, one female) said that they had been afraid and this prevented them from rising.

All floats and flights were stable and there were no accidents or problems with take-off or landing. Most subjects levitated with arms outstretched (as in free-fall) but two had no difficulty in flying with arms folded. All who flew said they thought that with practise they would be able to fly much higher and much farther. There was no difference in flight performance between those who were given the original pills and those who had the new pills.

A female flyer and both non-flyers complained of feeling slightly sick for about ten minutes after taking the pills. Three flyers said that they experienced a feeling of spiritual well-being both during and after flight, while others said that after the first shock of being able to levitate they found the experience exciting. The subjects were medically examined before and after each flight and no changes were noted in their physical condition.

Our observations leave no doubt that flights took place as a result of the levitation pill. There was no evidence to indicate how this apparent defiance of the laws of physics occurred, except that it might be connected with a 'will to believe', which could have mind–body implications.

Civil Aviation Act (1979)

> **Clause 2, Section B**
>
> The flight, or intended flight, by any aircraft, glider, balloon or other flying apparatus or machine may be undertaken only if the operator has been granted a licence from the Air Safety Council of Alpha.

Alpha Times - Obituary notice

> MISS MARIE LAL, who died last week at the age of 65, was a well-loved personality, but had eccentric habits. She always wore red and always carried two umbrellas – 'One for sun, one for rain'. She started her career as a chemist and, shortly before her death, claimed to have invented a pill that would, as she put it, 'allow people to rise up'. She refused to demonstrate the alleged pill, saying that it would not be polite to do so. She left most of her money to Alphatown Cats Home.

Alpha Scholastic Dictionary

> **levitātion** *n.* The rising and floating of heavy bodies in the air by non-physical means. (Latin: *levis*, light). Levitate, *v.* To rise, to make light, to achieve levitation.

Recommendations form

30 *Ministries of labels*

Description In this simulation participants are in charge of four ministries in the Government of Beta that have been requested to state what they actually do in order to see whether money can be saved. The ministries can negotiate with each other.

Objectives To enhance the skills of diplomacy, negotiation, planning and team building.

Time and numbers The time required is about an hour and a half. If there are more than 20 participants consider whether to run the simulation as 2 parallel events. The minimum number is probably eight – four pairs – although it would be possible to drop one of the ministries and run the event with six participants. There is no maximum.

Resources
* Briefing sheet – one copy for each participant.
* Memo from the Prime Minister's Office – one copy for each Ministry.
* Ministry identification tags – one (or more) for each Ministry.
* Interdepartmental form – three or four for each group
* Scrap paper.

Method
1 Hand out the Briefing sheets – one copy to each participant.

2 Divide the participants at random into four groups as far apart as possible (perhaps in separate rooms) and hand out the Ministry identification tags at random.

3 Hand out the copies of the Memo from the Prime Minister's Office and the Interdepartmental forms. Retrieve all the Briefing sheets

4 Set a time for the start of the debriefing and make scrap paper available.

Debriefing It might be a good idea to start by having the ministries debriefing themselves and then the groups revealing to a joint meeting any hidden strategies, secret deals and points of significance.

The full session could examine the diplomatic skills. Was it a straightforward 'If you support us, we will support you' approach or was it more subtle? Did they say one thing but mean another?

Was the Ministry of Ministries perceived as being under a greater or lesser threat of closure than the other three ministries? Did any Ministry see itself as more important than the others? What sort of deals, if any, were arrived at?

How effective was the planning? Did they have a fallback position in case they could not achieve their main objective.

How harmonious was the team building? Did one person in a team monopolize the job of envoy, leaving the others to feel left out of the decision-making process? For example, if there were three in a team, each person could have been a specialist envoy to one Ministry only or the envoys could have been rotated. Were such matters discussed or planned? How was an envoy chosen?

In this simulation you are in charge of four ministries in the Government of Beta that have been requested to state what they actually do in order to see whether money can be saved. They are the Ministry of Labels, the Ministry of Definitions, the Ministry of Terminology and the Ministry of Ministries. You will meet in your own Ministry to discuss the situation and you can negotiate with other ministries if you wish.

The situation is that a new government has just been elected. One of its election promises, expressed in very general terms, was to save taxpayers' money by reducing government bureaucracy. The outgoing Government had set up the Ministry of Labels, the Ministry of Definitions and the Ministry of Terminology in order to improve efficiency, to reduce misunderstandings and to clarify and simplify the complexities of modern life. At the same time, the Ministry of Ministries was set up to act as a watchdog and to coordinate and improve the work of other ministries and make them more accountable to the public. The current situation is that your Ministry has received a Memo from the Prime Minister's Office and a reply must be written on an Interdepartmental form.

You can meet with other ministries if you wish, on the following conditions:

* only one envoy from a Ministry is allowed to be on a visit at any one time
* if turned away, the envoy must not approach other ministries or engage in espionage, but must return immediately and report
* any deal or agreement between ministries is automatically confidential and must be written on an Interdepartmental form, signed by all staff of the two ministries concerned and placed in a secret safe (given to the facilitator).

Prime Minister's Office

MEMO

From: Personal Private Secretary to the Prime Minister

To: Ministry of Definitions
Ministry of Labels
Ministry of Terminology
Ministry of Ministries

The Prime Minister requests you to clarify the functions of your Ministry. Please:

1 explain, specify and describe what your Ministry does and
2 put forward suggestions for improving efficiency and saving money.

May I add a personal note – if your replies produce conflicting claims about your work, then the Prime Minister's advisers may suggest to the Prime Minister that this confirms the need to close some or all of your ministries.

----------- fold here -----------

Ministry of Definitions

----------- fold here -----------

Ministry of Labels

----------- fold here -----------

Ministry of Terminology

----------- fold here -----------

Ministry of Ministries

Interdepartmental form

Communication between:

_____

Contents:

_____

_____

_____

_____

_____

_____

_____

_____

_____

_____

_____

_____

31 *Real real*

Description   This is a simulation about planning a quest for the Real real.

Objectives   To enhance the skills of planning and team building.

Time and numbers   The time required is about half an hour for small numbers and more than an hour for large numbers. If numbers do not divide equally by four, then add a role for journalist (manager, observer, etc.). The minimum number is four. There is no maximum.

Resources
* Briefing sheet – one copy for each participant.
* Job tags – four for each group.
* Letter from Lord Delta – one copy for each participant.
* Vision sheet – one copy for each participant.
* Scrap paper.

Method
1 Hand out the Briefing sheets – one copy to each participant. If there is more than one group, you could mark the Briefing sheets so as to divide them into groups at random. Hand out to each group, face down, the Job tags and ask the participants to pick their own.

2 Hand out the copies of the Letter from Lord Delta and the Vision sheet – one copy of each to each participant. Allow participants a few minutes to think themselves into their roles as individuals before meeting the others. (You might ask them to stand up and assume that they are alone and are just entering one of Lord Delta's limousines to take them to the hotel.)

3 Retrieve the Briefing sheets. Set a time limit.

4 Make the scrap paper available.

5 If you could arrange for refreshments to be brought to the group during the action, this could enhance plausibility.

Debriefing   Depending on the numbers, it might be a good idea for each group to debrief themselves.

A meeting of all groups could begin with a brief account from each group of what ideas were accepted and rejected. Did any group arrive at any plausible concept of what the Real real might be or where it could be found or did they conclude that it was semantic nonsense? Did the Vision sheets read like business reports or messages of hope? Did the language reflect any of the enthusiasm of Lord Delta? Was there any difference between what they *thought* and what they *wrote*?

Did individuals think themselves into their occupations? How convincing were they in their expertise? Did they combine their specialities into a team?

How did they organize themselves? Did they set some sort of agenda or elect someone to the chair? Did they divide up the issues? Did they work as individuals or as sub-committees or as a committee? Did they look at the real world and discuss any examples and precedents?

On what issues were they most in agreement or disagreement? Did they produce an agreed plan or individual plans?

Did the participants build into their plans a provision for their own continuing responsibility (and payment) for the shaping and implementation of their ideas? Did they propose that they become an established team with a title, rather than remaining as separate individuals.

This is a simulation about planning a quest for the Real real.

You are an Historian, a Novelist, a Publicity Manager and a Psychologist. You have all accepted an invitation from Lord Delta, a newspaper and television tycoon, to participate in a one-day feasibility study about a quest for the Real real. You meet in the penthouse suite of a luxury hotel. Each person will receive a fee of £5000 plus an extra £5000 if Lord Delta is satisfied with your efforts.

You will have a Letter from Lord Delta, plus a Vision sheet on which to summarize your basic ideas. You can have more Vision sheets if you need them. Scrap paper is also available.

----------- fold here -----------

Historian

----------- fold here -----------

Novelist

----------- fold here -----------

Publicity Manager

----------- fold here -----------

Psychologist

Delta House

From: Lord Delta

I am most grateful to all of you for accepting my invitation to carry out a feasibility study into a quest for the Real real. I apologize that you are isolated in the penthouse suite, but you can order whatever you need in the way of food and refreshment. You can finish your task as early as you wish, but you must complete the study before 8 p.m. Fax the results to my office. Try to work as a team and produce one Vision sheet, but if you cannot agree, then set out your ideas individually on separate Vision sheets.

The Real real is just one further step along the road from the real thing, the real McCoy, the real self, the real truth. The Real real is the ultimate. It is the vision, the holy grail, the essence of reality, the crusade, the movement, the meaning. For many years I have felt its presence. It is like a bright illumination, but I find I cannot turn my head to see the source of the light. I have chosen you because you have the business sense, the knowledge, the imagination and the understanding of human beings to delve into this mystery.

I hope you can produce a vision, a challenge, a dream, an enlightenment, a philosophy, a movement, a mission or even a religion. If your work is successful, I will see that adequate resources are made available for a campaign. Nothing is too good for a mission that can lead people to the Real real.

What is the true nature of the Real real? Where can it be found? What do people have to do to find it? How can a campaign be organized?   Seek answers to questions and seek questions to answer.

Vision sheet

32 *Rollercoaster*

Description   This is a simulation in which teams design and build the last section of a paper rollercoaster.

Objectives   To enhance the skills of planning, problem solving, team building, time management and presentation.

Time and numbers   The time required is about an hour for small numbers and up to two hours for large numbers. The minimum number is about six and there is no maximum.

Resources
* Briefing sheet – one copy for each participant.
* Memo from Theme Park – one copy for each participant.
* Materials for each group:
  * 10 sheets of paper, plus glue
  * one one-foot (30-cm) ruler, one pair of scissors and a pen
  * one coin, which represents the car
  * scrap paper (for design and experiment, not construction).
* Identification tags – one for each organization.
* Self-assessment sheet – one copy for each participant (see suggestions in **Debriefing** section).

Method

1 Before the event begins, prepare packages of the Materials needed and work out (at least roughly) the size and number of groups. With five participants there could be two Construction teams, each with two members (the two other companies having dropped out), plus one participant in the role of Theme Park executive. With 24 participants there could be 4 Construction teams of 5 participants (or 5 teams of 4) and a team of 4 Theme Park executives. Allocate the participants into teams at random, then place the Identification tags face down and ask teams to pick their own.

2 The geographical location of chairs, tables and the presentation area(s) could be important because of the need to have as level a surface as possible. If the presentation area is different to the construction area(s), consider in advance the question of transport. It would be unfair if the teams had to construct their devices without realizing the need to move them to a presentation area. Also, there should be a special area where the Theme Park executives can meet in private to discuss their procedures.

3 Retrieve the Briefing sheets. Hand out the copies of the Memo from the Theme Park – one to each participant. Hand out the Materials to the Theme Park executives for them to pass on to the Construction companies. Fix a time for the end of the event.

Debriefing   This is one of the Five simple events listed in the Introduction and the easiest way to debrief a simple event is to ask the participants to fill in the Self-assessment sheets individually and use the results as a basis for discussion. The alternative is to take a more flexible approach and tailor the debriefing according to the particular course, the type of participants and significant episodes that occurred during the action. The following questions and suggestions could be used as a guide not only for the debriefing but also as a check-list of the sorts of things you could watch for in the action itself. (See also **Running the debriefing**, Introduction.)

As everyone will have seen the demonstrations and presentations, little time need be spent on discussing the merits of each construction – unless, of course, the participants are engaged in design or construction in real life.

A starting point could be a factual explanation by each construction team of the abandoned first thoughts, the process of decision making, how they allocated their time and, particularly, how much time was spent on planning the presentations.

The subsequent joint discussion is likely to be about the processes – the planning, problem solving, team building, time management and presentation. How well did the teams cooperate within themselves? Did the Theme Park staff work well with the Construction teams and vice versa?

Did Construction teams form any plan or did individuals simply pick up sheets of paper and start bending, folding and gluing? Was there any brainstorming or search for options or was the first plausible idea instantly adopted? Did they discuss who could work best with their hands?

Was there any discussion of timing or did they rush at the job? Did they consider the need to allocate sufficient time for discussing the way they should present their work? Did one person present the work or was it done as a team? Were the presentations confident and authoritative or were there merely a few inaudible remarks followed by a nervous dropping of the coin onto the model?

Did the Theme Park executives organize themselves with purpose and conviction or sit back and hope for the best? Did they visit each team at various stages of construction? How did they choose the order in which the teams should give their demonstrations? Did they show imagination in envisaging what might happen and what could go wrong? Did they arrange for a question and answer session after each presentation or did this option never occur to them? Did they give the Construction teams any guidance about how they should behave and where they should sit when watching the demonstrations?

What did the Theme Park executives think of the Construction teams and vice versa?

This is a simulation in which teams design and build the last section of a paper rollercoaster.

You are either executives of the Alphatown Theme Park or are executives of Construction companies seeking a contract to build a rollercoaster.

The Memo from the Theme Park explains what is required. The Theme Park executives are in charge of the assessment test. They will provide what is needed, will arrange the order in which the Construction companies give their presentations and will be in charge of timing. The Theme Park executives cannot allow the event to overrun as the room is needed later for a hospitality party for overseas visitors.

Alphatown Theme Park

To: Fairground Construction Company Ltd
Entertainment Enterprises
Rides and Slides
Funfairs Development Inc.

Our judgement is that all four companies could build the rollercoaster to the required safety standards and at a suitable price. However, we are looking for that extra bit of flair and imagination, plus an ability to tackle unexpected difficulties and to work well as a team, so we invite you to participate in an unusual event – to design and construct the final section of a rollercoaster using only paper and glue. We hope you will find the task enjoyable, challenging and, perhaps, educational.

Materials: 10 sheets of paper, plus glue.
Tools: One one-foot (30-cm) ruler, one pair of scissors and a pen.
Car: One coin, which represents the car.
Scrap paper: For design and experimental purposes only.

Specifications

1 The ride must include at least one uphill section.
2 The track can be either straight or curved or both.
3 The car (coin) can roll or slide or do both.
4 The construction must be freestanding and not glued to the surface.
5 Neither the tools nor the scrap paper can be incorporated into the construction.
6 When demonstrating your model, you will be allowed three runs of the car.

Judging

We shall look favourably on imaginative features, on thrills, variety and on a slow speed at the end of the ride. If the ride is dull or if the coin shoots off at speed at the end, we shall be less impressed.

If your coin becomes stuck on the way down or falls off the track or if the construction comes unstuck, this does not necessarily mean that you have failed to win the contract. We shall be watching the way you work as a team and may come round and ask you questions while you are on the job. We will be impressed by an authoritative presentation, perhaps mentioning the problems and difficulties encountered. We shall be less than enthusiastic if your team stands and says nothing and simply drops the coin on the top of the ride.

Our executives will give their comments immediately after the demonstrations. However, the final decision about the contract will take several days. We have a number of projects in the planning stage and if you are not offered the contract for the rollercoaster, it may be that we would approach you regarding other new rides.

Alphatown Theme Park

Fairground Construction Company Limited

Entertainment Enterprises

Rides and Slides

Funfairs Development Inc.

How did you begin? For example, did you start by working independently? Did you have a brainstorming session? Did you start by discussing options? Did you consider the time factor?

Looking back, did you give too much attention to one aspect? For example, did the Construction teams concentrate on design and neglect presentation or work on their own ideas and neglect other people's suggestions? Did the Theme Park executives concentrate on observing and neglect the task of devising clear procedures for the presentations?

Did you allocate different jobs? For example, did you make someone the boss? Did you put someone in charge of keeping an eye on the time?

How did you handle disagreements?

How effective were the presentations and the assessments? Did the design teams simply place the coin on the device and fail to mention what had happened in the design process? Did the Theme Park executives give a good summing up?

How do you assess yourself?

Skills	Poor	Fair	Good	Excellent
Creativity				
Planning				
Presentation				
Problem solving				
Team building				
Time management				
(Other)				

How do you assess your team?

Skills	Poor	Fair	Good	Excellent
Creativity				
Planning				
Presentation				
Problem solving				
Team building				
Time management				
(Other)				

Efficiency areas

33 *Anagram scores*

Description

This is an exercise in which participants have to prepare for three minutes of action during which they try to form words from nine letters. Each team chooses one of three groups of letters during its preparation and the scores depend not on the number or length of the words but on how many pre-chosen letters they contain.

Objectives

To enhance the skills of planning, problem solving, team building and time management.

Time and numbers

With small groups, allow half an hour. With 20 or more participants divided into several teams, allow about an hour because of the need to explain, compare and comment on different groups' work in the debriefing. The minimum number is about three. There is no maximum.

Resources

* Briefing sheet – one copy for each participant.
* Scoring letters A – one copy for each team (handed out only if chosen).
* Scoring letters B – one copy for each team (handed out only if chosen).
* Scoring letters C – one copy for each team (handed out only if chosen).
* Working letters – one copy for facilitator.
* Any timepiece with a second hand, the larger the better.
* Scrap paper.

Method

1 Before beginning, cut out each of the three sets of Scoring letters. If you have several teams, prepare three sets for each team, just in case each team chooses the same set.

2 Hand out the Briefing sheets – one to each participant – and divide the participants at random into three groups. If there are more than about 20 participants, it may be a good idea to appoint a second facilitator and run the exercise as 2 parallel events.

3 Retrieve the Briefing sheets and set a time for the start of the joint word building session.

4 Hand out the Scoring letters A or B or C as requested by each team.

5 For the word building session, arrange the three groups so that they have a clear view of you when you display the Working letters.

6 When it comes to adding up the scores, watch out for words with repeated letters (dated, edited, addict, account) that are ineligible.

7 Note that the length of the word does not affect the score. Thus, for a team that chooses set A Scoring letters (A D G J M P T W), the word 'ounce' would score nil, whereas 'date' would score three and 'tad' (to spread out, scatter or strew) would also score three.

Debriefing

It could be a good idea for the teams to debrief themselves and then explain and discuss at a joint session the way they planned their problem solving, team building and time management.

The answer to the nine-letter anagram that earned five bonus points is 'education'.

Each team's Scoring letters include three Working letters, as follows:

Scoring letters	Working letters
A D G J M P T W	A D T
B E H K N R U Y	E N U
C F I L O S V Z	C I O

This means that 'education' scores three points plus five extra bonus points for whichever team finds the word. The word 'dunce' would score one point for the team with A letters, three points for the team with B letters and one point for the team with C letters. Apart from 'education' no word can score more than three points because each team has only three Scoring letters available for word building.

Regarding the objectives of team building and time management, a key question to ask is whether the teams would organize themselves any differently if the event was rerun. How were decisions taken? Did anyone suggest breaking up the task of word building – for example, a team of three, each taking three of the nine letters as initial letters for word building. Did they assess their skills before they began? Did they appoint a timekeeper? Did they search for options or just work on the first idea to be suggested? How accurate were the final scores as a measure of efficient teamwork?

This is an exercise in which participants have to prepare for three minutes of action during which they try to form words from nine letters. Each team chooses one of three groups of letters during its preparation and the scores depend not on the number or length of the words but on how many pre-chosen letters they contain.

The exercise starts with a strategy session in which teams have plenty of time to choose letter packages A or B or C and work out procedures for the word building session.

Working letters

There are nine Working letters, none of which are repeated, and are an anagram of a nine-letter word. The nine letters will be displayed by the facilitator at the beginning of a three-minute period, during which the groups have the task of forming words of three or more letters from these nine letters alone.

Scoring letters

The letters Q and X are omitted and there a three groups of eight letters each. Each team must choose one of the following groups:

* Group A – every third letter of the alphabet, starting with A
* Group B – every third letter of the alphabet, starting with B
* Group C – every third letter of the alphabet, starting with C.

When your team has decided on its choice, tell the facilitator who will give you the package of letters (as proof of your request and to help you to work out procedures).

Word building

1 Each word must be a dictionary word of at least three letters.
2 Each word must be composed entirely of Working letters.
3 No letter can be repeated in a word because no letter is repeated in the nine.
4 The word building session will be a strictly timed three-minute period, starting from when the nine Working letters are displayed.

Scoring

1 One point for each Scoring letter used.
2 An extra five bonus points if the nine-letter anagram is solved.

Here is an example of how it works. Supposing a team builds a three-letter dictionary word from the nine Working letters, the score depends on how many of the team's Scoring letters it contains. If it contains no Scoring letters, the score is nil; if it has one Scoring letter, the score is one; if two, the score is two; and if all three letters are Scoring letters the score is three.

Scoring letters A: A   D   G   J   M   P   T   W

Scoring letters B: B   E   H   K   N   R   U   Y

Scoring letters C: C   F   I   L   O   S   V   Z

Scoring letters A: A   D   G   J   M   P   T   W

Scoring letters B: B   E   H   K   N   R   U   Y

Scoring letters C: C   F   I   L   O   S   V   Z

Scoring letters A: A   D   G   J   M   P   T   W

Scoring letters B: B   E   H   K   N   R   U   Y

Scoring letters C: C   F   I   L   O   S   V   Z

Working letters

A	C	D
E	I	N
O	T	U

34 *Eliminating words*

Description   This simulation is about a feasibility study in the Kingdom of Lexicona aimed at eliminating non-essential words from the vocabulary used for public communications.

Objectives   To enhance the skills of communication and team building in a context involving gender.

Time and numbers   With small numbers, allow up to an hour. With larger numbers allow about an hour and a half. The minimum number is four – two pairs and using only two of the four lists of words. With 20 participants, have 4 groups of 5 each. With more than 20 participants the simulation could be run as 2 parallel events. There is no maximum.

Resources
* Briefing sheet – one copy for each participant.
* Memo from the Ministry of Efficiency – one copy for each group.
* Word lists A, B, C and D – one list for each group (plus some spares).
* Scrap paper.

Method
1 To achieve random grouping, mark the Briefing sheets A, B, C or D, lay them face down and allow participants to pick their own.

2 Locate the groups in the four corners of the room in alphabetical sequence. (This will help the process of passing on the suggestions in a clockwise direction.)

3 Retrieve the Briefing sheets and hand out copies of the Memo from the Ministry of Efficiency – one to each group.

4 Hand out the Word lists A, B, C and D to the appropriate groups. (Keep some spares handy in case the participants have second thoughts about their answers.)

5 Hand out the scrap paper and set a time for passing the Word list to the next group for reappraisal.

Debriefing   Arrange for some procedure whereby each team takes it in turn to announce its conclusions and avoid discussing the issues arising until this has been done.

The discussion could concentrate on those areas of agreement or disagreement that are the most interesting or significant. Was disagreement purely semantic or did it involve judgements about gender and human values?

Was the fundamental idea sound – would a reduced working vocabulary reduce misunderstanding and inefficiency?

How effective was the communication and team building? Did each team operate as a committee or split up and give different word pairs to individuals? Did anyone take charge of the procedures? How did teams react to the other team's recommendations – was the attitude one of fault-finding or rubber stamping endorsement or impartial appraisal?

This simulation is about a feasibility study in the Kingdom of Lexicona aimed at eliminating non-essential words from the vocabulary used for public communications.

You will be in one of four groups – A, B, C or D – and will have a Memo from the Ministry of Efficiency. In addition, each group will receive one of four lists of word pairs – A, B, C, D. Having made choices, the list must be passed on to the next group in a clockwise direction at the time limit, even if decisions have not been made about all the words. The comments column is for the group that receives the list.

Please read the Memo carefully before starting to take decisions about the words.

Ministry of Efficiency

MEMO

To: Feasibility study groups

You have been chosen at random from the staff of the Ministry to take part in a feasibility study aimed at eliminating non-essential words from the vocabulary used in public communications. The purpose is to see to what extent it is possible to agree on which words to drop.

The aim is not to rewrite the dictionary, nor to ban certain words – it is not aimed at restricting people's private vocabularies. The aim is to improve the words selected for public communications. The objective is to produce a list of recommended words that can be published, made available to the public and circulated to all government departments, businesses, publishers, educational establishments and the media. If this could be done, it could facilitate understanding, increase efficiency, reduce misunderstandings and also make it easier and less expensive for people to learn the language.

With this Memo you will be receiving one of four lists of word pairs – A, B, C or D. It has two columns, one for your group and one for the group that appraises your list of choices. Do *not* write comments about your own choice of words.

The procedure is as follows:

* if the whole team agrees that a word should be kept, put a tick in the box after the word
* if the whole team agrees that a word should be dropped, put a cross in the box
* if the whole team cannot agree or cannot make up its mind about a word, put nothing
* two ticks for a pair means that *both* words should be kept
* two crosses for a pair (although unlikely) means *both* words should be dropped
* two blanks means the team is undecided about both words.

When you receive the list in the second stage, simply write in the comments column any comment that the team can agree on. If the team cannot agree, then write nothing.

Procedural advice

1 Go through the list quickly without taking decisions.
2 Go through it again and mark the words you agree on.
3 Spend the rest of the time trying to agree on as many words as possible, skipping words that cause more than a reasonable amount of disagreement.

Word list A

Choices			Comments
waiter	❑	waitress ❑	_____
			_____
sex	❑	gender ❑	_____
			_____
duty	❑	obligation ❑	_____
			_____
preservation	❑	conservation ❑	_____
			_____
spying	❑	espionage ❑	_____
			_____
timely	❑	opportune ❑	_____
			_____
idea	❑	thought ❑	_____
			_____
empty	❑	blank ❑	_____
			_____
likely	❑	probable ❑	_____
			_____
ability	❑	capability ❑	_____
			_____
plausible	❑	credible ❑	_____
			_____

Word list B

	Choices		Comments
actor	☐ actress	☐	_____
			_____
dozen	☐ twelve	☐	_____
			_____
ethics	☐ morals	☐	_____
			_____
uninterested	☐ disinterested	☐	_____
			_____
small	☐ little	☐	_____
			_____
business	☐ enterprise	☐	_____
			_____
speed	☐ velocity	☐	_____
			_____
stop	☐ halt	☐	_____
			_____
pompous	☐ pretentious	☐	_____
			_____
cooking	☐ cuisine	☐	_____
			_____
less	☐ fewer	☐	_____
			_____

Word list C

	Choices		Comments
humans	☐ mankind	☐	_____
			_____
shepherd	☐ shepherdess	☐	_____
			_____
god	☐ goddess	☐	_____
			_____
freedom	☐ liberty	☐	_____
			_____
help	☐ aid	☐	_____
			_____
stomach	☐ abdomen	☐	_____
			_____
game	☐ simulation	☐	_____
			_____
delete	☐ erase	☐	_____
			_____
foresee	☐ predict	☐	_____
			_____
clock	☐ chronometer	☐	_____
			_____
tool	☐ implement	☐	_____
			_____

Word list D

	Choices		**Comments**
hero	❑ heroine	❑	_____
milkman	❑ milkmaid	❑	_____
lawful	❑ legal	❑	_____
aims	❑ objectives	❑	_____
sure	❑ certain	❑	_____
lucky	❑ fortunate	❑	_____
amusement	❑ entertainment	❑	_____
stupid	❑ silly	❑	_____
alert	❑ vigilant	❑	_____
prefer	❑ favour	❑	_____
midday	❑ noon	❑	_____

35 *Fungus*

Description

A simulation in which Managers of a large supermarket have to deal with the problem of a fungus that appears to grow on the working surfaces of computers in its Accounts and Sales Departments.

Objectives

To enhance the skills of communication, planning and team building.

Time and numbers

With small numbers the time required would probably be about half an hour. With ten or more participants, and using several groups, about an hour should be allowed so that the debriefing can be used to describe, compare and comment upon the actions of the groups. The minimum number is four. There is no maximum.

Resources

* Briefing sheet – one copy for each participant.
* Four Job tags – one set for each group.
* Memo from the Administrative Manager – one copy for each participant.
* Scrap paper.

Method

1 Depending on the numbers, divide the participants into groups of four, perhaps by marking the Briefing sheets, laying them face down and allowing the participants to pick their own. If the numbers do not divide equally by four, some jobs can be shared (a colleague from the same department) or remaining participants can fulfill the role of observer(s).

2 Retrieve the Briefing sheets and hand out the Job tags, perhaps by placing them on the table face down and asking the participants to pick their own.

3 Hand out the Memo from the Administrative Manager.

4 Set a time for the start of the debriefing.

5 Make scrap paper available.

Debriefing

If there is more than one group, it might be a good idea for each group to debrief themselves. This can be followed by a meeting of all groups, beginning with a brief account from each group of what ideas were accepted and rejected.

There is no hidden answer to the fungus question, it is a mystery. Perhaps it is harmless and will disappear, perhaps it has something to do with the air conditioning, perhaps it presages an invasion from outer space! How did the participants cope with a mystery? Whether they decided to do something or nothing about the fungus, did they discuss whether they should reveal what they knew? Did they decide to write a memo, interview people personally, call in government biologists or tell the story to the local media? Did anyone decide privately to earn money by selling the story to the media?

Did they search for options or simply discuss the first plausible course of action to be suggested? Did they plan effectively or haphazardly? Did they assume the worst possible case or the best possible case? Did anyone write anything (or draw anything) on the scrap paper?

Did they draw up contingency plans, working out who should get in touch with whom if the fungus spread or if the staff became alarmed.

How well did they communicate? How well did they work as a team? Did they take account of their own departmental responsibilities? Did they consider other people's Departments? Did they consider the possibility of a contamination scare? Did anyone show imagination and innovative thinking?

How effective was the team building? Did anyone take charge of the proceedings? How did they handle disagreements?

This is a simulation in which a large supermarket has encountered a fungus on the working surfaces of computers in its Accounts and Sales Departments.

You will have one of four functional roles – General Manager, Financial Manager, Personnel Manager, Sales Manager. The Administrative Manager, who will not be present at the meeting, has left a Memo that explains the situation.

----------- fold here -----------

General Manager

----------- fold here -----------

Financial Manager

----------- fold here -----------

Personnel Manager

----------- fold here -----------

Sales Manager

MEMO

From: Administrative Manager
To: General Manager, Financial Manager, Personnel Manager and Sales Manager

A week ago the working surfaces and keyboards of the computers in the Accounts and Sales Departments began to be covered with a thin, grey film that appeared overnight and has continued to appear. The computer operators, thinking it to be dust, simply wiped it away before beginning work. However, one elderly operator expressed her dislike for the dust and I granted her temporary leave, which, together with some holiday leave that was owing, means that she has now retired.

I personally took a sample of the grey film and passed it on to an acquaintance who is a senior biologist at the University. She stated that the substance is not dust, but a fungus, saying 'It is a plant lacking in chlorophyll that reproduces by spores'. She said it was most unlikely, if not impossible, that the fungus could 'grow' on the plastic surface of the computers, but suggested that we should inspect them carefully to see if there was any fungus inside. She said that the probable cause was the ventilation system or perhaps a sharp variation between the interior and exterior temperatures or, perhaps, a night-time cloud of dampness. She said that there was nothing to suggest that the fungus could have any harmful effect on health. It was not toxic in any way and, as fungus in general is a somewhat erratic organism, the phenomena would probably disappear of its own accord. Meanwhile, she is treating the matter in confidence.

I inspected the interior of a couple of computers without mentioning the reason and I could find no traces at all of any fungus. There was no trace of the fungus on any other plastic surfaces. A new computer terminal, installed only yesterday, attracted the same amount of fungus as the older computers. I carefully inspected our food department and found no fungus. The presence of the fungus seems to have no effect on anything. The staff in the computer room still assume that the substance is dust and wipe it off without fuss, although yesterday I overheard one operator make a remark to a colleague about the dust being a nuisance.

I am sorry I cannot be present at the meeting, but I feel sure that you will take whatever steps, if any, are necessary and I will consult with you on my return in a couple of weeks.

36 *Gender in law*

Description   A simulation set in the Republic of Delta where a private investigation by the largest law firm there has produced some unexpected evidence in relation to the way juries behave regarding gender. Participants are Senior partners in the firm.

Objectives   To enhance the skills of communication and team building in a context involving gender.

Time and numbers   With small numbers, the time required would be between half an hour and an hour. With larger numbers it would be an hour to an hour and a half. The minimum number is probably three or four and there is no maximum, but it is best to restrict the size of a group to four or five.

Resources
* Briefing sheet – one copy for each participant.
* Miss Epsilon's report – one copy for each participant.
* Scrap paper.

Method
1 With eight or more participants, run the event in parallel groups and, perhaps, mark the Briefing sheets to indicate the group, place the sheets face down and let the participants pick their own sheet.

2 Retrieve the Briefing sheets and hand out the copies of Miss Epsilon's report.

3 Make scrap paper available and set a time limit for the discussions.

Debriefing   If there is more than one group, each group could take it in turns to describe what happened in that group.

Did discussions within groups centre on the gender issue? Did the Senior partners communicate with each other objectively from the point of view of the law firm or treat the issues personally and emotionally?

Did the Senior partners search for options for decision making or debate equal rights in Delta? Did they tackle the question of whether it would be in the interests of the firm to disclose the findings? If they were in favour of disclosure, did they discuss how this should this be done and whether the firm should issue a statement on policy and make recommendations? If they were not in favour of disclosure, then what advice would be given to clients who had a choice between a court hearing and an out-of-court settlement? Did they discuss what answer should be given if a client asked for the reasoning behind the advice? Did they consider what they would do if they were later accused of a cover-up by concealing the report? How would they react to a newspaper story headlined 'Law firm conceals sex report'?

Note: Another simulation involving gender in Delta is event 40, Women managers.

This is a simulation set in the Republic of Delta where a private investigation by the largest law firm has produced some unexpected evidence in relation to the way juries behave.

You are a Senior partner in the law firm Alpha, Beta and Gamma that specializes in civil cases and you meet with your fellow lawyers to decide what should be done, if anything, about Miss Epsilon's report on jury behaviour. For example, you could decide to write a brief summary of the findings for the *Delta Law Journal*.

The Head of the Research Department of your firm, Miss Geraldine Epsilon, who compiled the report will not be present at your meeting. She is visiting the United States.

Alpha, Beta and Gamma
Deltatown

Strictly confidential – for Senior partners' eyes only

Report by Geraldine Epsilon, Head of Research Department

I was requested to conduct a confidential survey to ascertain whether jurors were biased in favour of people of their own sex when deciding cases and whether such a bias had any legal or social implications.

As juries reach their decisions in secret, I decided to conduct a survey of cases during the last five years that fulfilled the following three conditions:

1 only civil cases were included, not criminal cases
2 that a man and a woman were on opposite sides
3 that at least two thirds of the jury were of the same sex.

Out of thousands of cases there were just 286 that conformed to these conditions.
The findings were as follows.

Jury	Percentage in favour of	
	male	female
Predominantly male jury (147 cases)	52%	48%
Predominantly female jury (139 cases)	36%	64%

In the cases where there were predominantly female juries, the results were statistically significant, suggesting that the juries were biased in favour of females. In the cases where there were predominantly male juries, the results in favour of males were not statistically significant.

Regarding legal significance, the findings may affect the advice we give to clients. Regarding social significance it is impossible to do other than speculate. One possibility is that women jurors, consciously or unconsciously, may be trying to redress what they perceive, rightly or wrongly, as unfair treatment of Deltan women. Only in the last five years have women been given equal opportunities for jury service. Unlike many other countries, there is no legislation in Delta for equal opportunities and human rights, apart from common law provisions regarding equality before the law and the concept of fair dealing. Another possibility is that the findings, although statistically significant, might still have occurred as a result of chance factors unconnected with gender.

On the question of confidentiality, I personally worked out the statistics from the raw data and have informed no one else of the findings.

37 *Helpers*

Description

A simulation involving people being trained in counselling at the Government's Health at Work Agency. The trainees take on the roles of Managers, Workers and Counsellors in construction tasks using paper. This simulation has a hidden agenda, namely that, although everyone is informed that the Workers require precise instructions, the Workers themselves are told not to help by making intelligent guesses about ambiguous and imprecise instructions and are paid higher rates for overtime after five minutes.

Objectives

To enhance the skills of communication, counselling, planning, problem solving and team building.

Time and numbers

With small numbers the simulation will take about half an hour. With larger numbers an hour should be allowed. The minimum number is four – one Manager, two Workers and one Counsellor. There is no maximum.

Resources

* Briefing sheet – one copy for each participant.
* Managers' task sheet – one copy for each Manager.
* Workers' task sheet – one copy for each Worker.
* Counsellors' task sheet – one copy for each Counsellor.
* Paper – rectangular, not square and about the size of A4 – several sheets for each group of Workers. (Although the task requires only one sheet it may become damaged so each group of Workers should have spare sheets available.)
* Ruler, scissors, pen – one of each for each group of Workers.
* Scrap paper for Managers and Counsellors.
* Self-assessment sheet – one copy for each participant (see suggestions in **Debriefing** section).

Method

1 In dividing up the jobs, always have at least two Workers and not more than three. With eight participants it could be run as two events or as a single event with perhaps three Managers, three Workers and two Counsellors. If you run the events in parallel it is important to have ample space between the events as orders will be given verbally and perhaps noisily.

2 If there are parallel events, the Briefing sheets could be marked with the job and the group and placed face down, letting the participants pick their own sheet.

3 Hand out the Managers', Workers' and Counsellors' task sheets to the appropriate groups. Give the Workers' group(s) the paper, rulers, scissors and pens.

4 Retrieve the Briefing sheets. Allow the participants time to discuss the situation in their own groups. Set a deadline for the start of the construction task.

5 Allow 10-20 minutes for the construction. You have the option of either specifying the time allowed (preferably not less than ten minutes) or setting no time limit, apart from saying that the work should be neither rushed nor treated leisurely.

6 After the construction task, the Counsellors should comment (within the event) on what they observed and state whether they would recommend counselling procedures to deal with stress.

Debriefing

This is one of the Five simple events listed in the Introduction and the easiest way to debrief a simple event is to ask the participants to fill in the Self-assessment sheets individually and use the results as a basis for discussion. The alternative is to take a more flexible approach and tailor the debriefing according to the particular course, the type of participants and significant episodes that occurred during the action. The following questions and suggestions could be used as a guide not only for the debriefing but also as a check-list of the sorts of things you could watch for in the action itself. (See also **Running the debriefing**, Introduction.)

Start by revealing the hidden agenda. You, or the Workers, should read out (and not just summarize) the instructions. It may be that in the course of the construction the Managers did not tell the Workers the objectives, simply giving instructions, and in this case the Managers' objectives could be read out. The Counsellors should explain what their instructions were.

In the subsequent joint discussion, one area to explore is the degree of planning and team building within each group and the communication between Managers and Workers.

Did Managers tell the Workers the objectives – as distinct from giving them orders? Did they say 'The object is to produce the largest possible square and cut it out' or did they say 'Get hold of the right-hand corner of the long side and fold it over'? Did any Manager encourage the Workers or praise them? Were the instructions friendly or formal? Did the Workers obey their own secret instructions or take delight in sabotaging the work of the Managers?

Did stress occur? How did the groups cope with this? Did anyone get upset and, if so, did other team members try to calm things down? Did the Counsellors impose a cooling off period?

Was the summing up by the Counsellors appropriate to the context of the training of people for the job of Counsellors in the Government's Health at Work Agency? Did the Counsellors take the opportunity to draw comparisons between the exercise and the real world of work, communication and stress?

This is a simulation in which you are people being trained in counselling at the Government's Health at Work Agency. As part of the training you take on the roles of Managers, Workers and Counsellors in construction tasks using paper.

Only the Workers can touch the materials. The Managers are not allowed to touch the materials. The Managers are required to give precise instructions to the Workers about what is required. All instructions must be verbal. Managers are not allowed to use scrap paper to demonstrate what is required.

The Workers must carry out all instructions that are precise.

The Counsellors have the job of noting and assessing communication problems and have the authority to call for a two-minute cooling off period if a situation becomes unduly heated. After the construction task is finished, they have the job of summarizing what they observed.

The construction requirements are contained in the Managers' and Counsellors' task sheets. The Workers' task sheet contains only guidelines.

Managers' task sheet

The task involves one (or more) sheets of paper and the tools are a ruler, a pen and a pair of scissors. Only Workers may touch these materials and tools. You must not touch any materials or tools or use paper to demonstrate what is required.

Your task is to issue precise instructions to the Workers to achieve the following:

1 produce the largest possible square from a sheet of paper and cut it out

2 divide the square into two equal-sized triangles marked A and B and cut them out

3 fold A once so that it has two parallel sides

4 fold B and, perhaps, cut B so that it becomes a dart

5 from chest height, launch the dart to achieve a reasonably stable forward glide – three launch attempts are permitted.

Before you start, it is a good idea to work out a few precise instructions and logical sequences and to decide who should do what in your team.

Workers' task sheet

The task involves one (or more) sheets of paper and the tools are a ruler, a pen and a pair of scissors. The Managers have the job of giving you precise instructions to perform various tasks.

You are paid by the time taken to achieve your task and you will get the overtime rate if the task lasts for more than five minutes. You are not allowed to slack or go slow or deliberately provoke the Managers, but you have a financial incentive not to assist the Managers by making intelligent guesses about instructions that are ambiguous or unclear.

You have various options:

1 you can make suggestions – for example, if ordered to draw a line on the paper, you could suggest to the Managers that one of you should hold the ruler while another draws the line

2 you can ask for clarification – for example, if ordered to draw a line, you could ask what sort of line, how thick and who should draw it; you could ask the Managers to rephrase their instructions

3 you can take action that obeys the instructions but does not entail a contribution of intelligence on your part to interpret what the Managers have in mind – for example, if asked to draw a line, you could draw a wavy line incorporating a few artistic circles; if asked to cut something out, you could do it carefully or carelessly, slowly or quickly, well or badly or have a discussion about who should hold the scissors.

Before you start it is a good idea to think of a few hypothetical instructions and decide how you would behave. However, your role is not that of clown or saboteur. Do not argue. Do as you are told. Do not grin at the Managers if they become upset. Be sympathetic, be polite, be respectful and always be ready to make helpful suggestions.

Counsellors' task sheet

The task involves one (or more) sheets of paper and the tools are a ruler, a pen and a pair of scissors. Your job is to observe the behaviour of the Managers and Workers during the construction task. After the task is completed, you will be expected to say a few words about behaviour (particularly any stress) and mention whether or not you would recommend counselling.

You are not allowed to visit the Managers or Workers before the task. You are not allowed to touch any of the materials or tools. You are not allowed to interfere with the task, but you can call for a two-minute cooling off period if you think that people have become too upset. You should discuss among yourselves what you will be looking for. At the end of the construction task your job is to summarize what you observed and comment on its connection with communication, stress and counselling.

To help you understand what you will see, the Managers have been told to issue 'precise instructions' to the Workers to achieve the following:

1 produce the largest possible square from a sheet of paper and cut it out

2 divide the square into two equal-sized triangles marked A and B and cut them out

3 fold A once so that it has two parallel sides

4 fold B and, perhaps, cut B so that it becomes a dart

5 from chest height, launch the dart to achieve a reasonably stable forward glide – three launch attempts are permitted.

How did you begin? For example, did you have a brainstorming session? Did you look at options? Did you work out plans for dealing with possible situations? Did you consider the time factor?

Did you allocate different jobs within your team? For example, did you make someone the boss? Did you decide who should do what?

How did you handle disagreements?

How did you handle stress? Did you counsel anyone within your own team?

In the summing up of the action, did the Counsellors refer to counselling?

How do you assess yourself?

Skills	Poor	Fair	Good	Excellent
Efficiency				
Communication				
Counselling				
Planning				
Problem solving				
Team building				
(Other)				

How do you assess your team?

Skills	Poor	Fair	Good	Excellent
Efficiency				
Communication				
Counselling				
Planning				
Problem solving				
Team building				
(Other)				

38 *Sports edition*

Description	A simulation set in the Republic of Remote where the population of the villages are keen to buy the sports edition of whichever of the two local newspapers delivers first. Each newspaper – the *Remote Drum* and the *Remote Trumpet* – has two delivery trucks, both owned independently, and the owners are paid according to the number of sales. Within each newspaper the Truck owners can negotiate their routes between themselves.
Objectives	To enhance the skills of negotiation, planning and problem solving.
Time and numbers	The event should take about half an hour with small numbers and up to an hour with large numbers because more time will be required for explaining, comparing and discussing skills and strategies in the debriefing. The minimum number is four – each participant being a Truck owner. With eight participants, there could be two people in each truck or it could be run as two parallel events, each with four participants. There is no maximum number.
Resources	✳ Briefing sheet – one copy for each participant. ✳ Map of the villages – one copy for each Truck owner, with spares available. ✳ Delivery schedule – one copy for each Truck owner (or Truck crew). ✳ Scrap paper and coloured pens. ✳ Self-assessment sheet – one copy for each participant (see suggestions in **Debriefing** section).
Method	**1** Divide the participants into teams of between one and four participants in each team to represent a Truck owner. To achieve a random distribution of groups, you could mark the Briefing sheets, lay them face down and let the participants pick their own.
	2 It is important that Truck owners should not deliberately or accidentally observe the markings on the Map or the Delivery schedule of their rivals, so keep teams from different newspapers as far apart as possible. If you have two rooms available and are running the simulation as two or three parallel events, you could have *Remote Drum* teams in one room and *Remote Trumpet* teams in the other.
	3 Hand out copies of the Map of the villages and the Delivery schedule – one copy of each to each team.
	4 Retrieve the Briefing sheets. Set a deadline for completing the Delivery schedule. Make the scrap paper available and hand out the coloured pens to enable teams to draw easily distinguishable routes on the Map. Explain, too, that spare copies of the Map are available should a team have second thoughts about its route.
Debriefing	This is one of the Five simple events listed in the Introduction and the easiest way to debrief a simple event is to ask the participants to fill in the Self-assessment sheets individually and use the results as a basis for discussion. The alternative is to take a more flexible approach and tailor the debriefing according to the particular course, the type of participants and significant episodes that occurred during the action. The following questions and suggestions could be used as a guide not only for the debriefing but also as a

check-list of the sorts of things you could watch for in the action itself. (See also **Running the debriefing**, Introduction.)

At the end of the simulation, work out the wages for each Truck owner. One way of doing this is to use a spare copy of the Map (or perhaps produce a large display map) and have four different colours to mark the routes. First draw all four routes from M to the first village on each route. If all four villages are different, then each team will have earned two Rems, but if two arrive at a village simultaneously they will have one Rem each. Do the same for the next village on each route and so on until the twelfth village.

It is a good idea to begin the discussion with each team giving the inside story of its strategy and explaining whether they cooperated with the truck serving the same newspaper and, if so, whether they sought a strategy that might benefit themselves more than their colleagues? Did any two owners agree to pool their earnings and share them on a 50–50 basis (the Briefing sheet refers to the options of negotiating routes 'and any other matters')?

Once each team has explained the background information and divulged any secret thoughts, the discussion could (briefly) examine the question of whether it was better to divide the Map one way rather than another – for example, was a north/south division more profitable than an inner/outer division? How did each Truck owner (or Truck crew) tackle the problem?

A key issue is the negotiation procedures. To what extent did each Truck owner seek to negotiate a division of territory with the Truck owner delivering the same newspaper? If there were two or more crew in each truck, then how did each truck's team cooperate among themselves? What did they do if there was disagreement? Would they do it any differently when faced with the delivery of the next sports editions?

This is a simulation set in a small Third World country, the Republic of Remote. You have the role of the Truck owners (and perhaps the Truck crews) who deliver the sports edition of the two local newspapers, the *Remote Drum* and the *Remote Trumpet.*

The population of the villages are so keen to buy the sports edition that they have no loyalty to either paper. They all buy from the first truck to arrive. This means that the second (or third, or fourth) truck reaching the village sells no papers.

The *Remote Trumpet* and *Remote Drum* each hire two trucks. Truck owner-drivers are independent and are paid as follows:

* two Rems if the truck is the first to arrive at the village
* no Rems if the village has already been visited
* if the village has not been visited and two (or more) trucks arrive simultaneously the two Rems are shared.

Within each newspaper, the two Truck owners can, if they so wish, negotiate their routes and any other matters between themselves. The coloured pens can be used to plot the two routes on the Map of the villages.

All routes start from M, the main town in Remote, which is where the two papers are printed. Around M are 24 villages, linked by road to their nearest neighbours. Each truck sets off at the same time and travels at the same speed. Each truck is expected to visit 12 villages. Once the route for a truck has been plotted, the Delivery schedule must be filled in and handed to the newspaper office (the facilitator) before any trucks set out.

Teams are forbidden to contact the teams working for the rival paper. They would be seen doing this, would lose their contracts and probably be charged with fraud. Do not wander into the vicinity of rival teams, hoping to observe their routes as anyone found guilty of industrial espionage in Remote receives a heavy prison sentence.

At the end of the simulation, the earnings of each Truck owner will be determined by plotting the movements of the four trucks and working out the earnings village by village.

Map of the villages

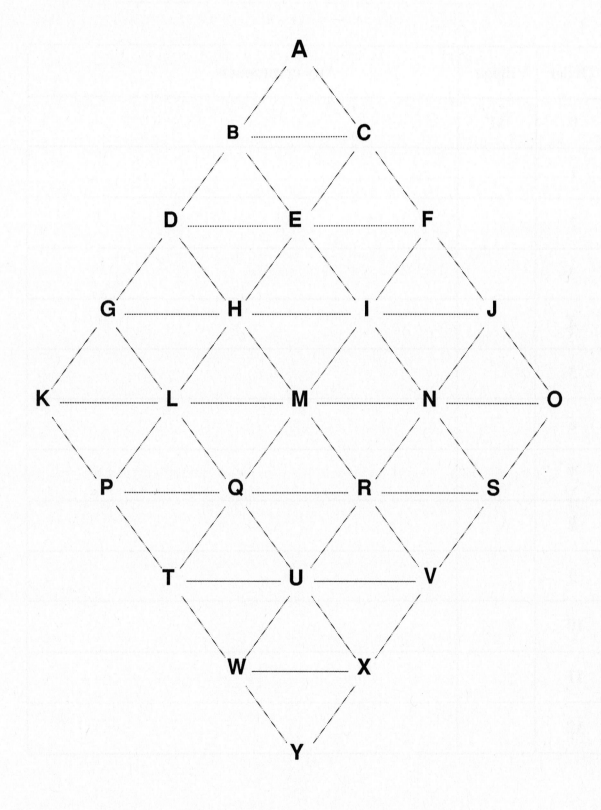

Delivery schedule

Truck owner: _____

Order	Village	Any comments
0	M	
1		
2		
3		
4		
5		
6		
7		
8		
9		
10		
11		
12		

How did you begin? For example, did you start with a brainstorming session? Did you start by discussing options?

Did you cooperate or compete with the other Truck owner who was delivering the same newspaper?

If you cooperated, did you consider anything other than a north-south division of territory? Did you look at the possibility of an inner-outer division or of 'jumping forward' to try to get one or two villages ahead of the opposition?

Did you consider pooling your earnings with the other Truck owner and dividing the money on a 50–50 basis?

How did you negotiate? Did you have any secret strategies?

How did you handle disagreements?

How do you assess yourself?

Skills	Poor	Fair	Good	Excellent
Efficiency				
Negotiation				
Planning				
Problem solving				
(Other)				

How do you assess your team?

Skills	Poor	Fair	Good	Excellent
Efficiency				
Negotiation				
Planning				
Problem solving				
(Other)				

39 *Trading values*

Description

This is a game that starts with each player ranking five symbols in order of personal value. Players meet in pairs and Symbol cards are traded on a one-for-one basis. The official value of individual symbols can be fixed by agreement.

Objectives

To enhance the skills of diplomacy, negotiation, planning and problem solving.

Time and numbers

Allow up to an hour with small numbers and more than an hour with large numbers, because of the extra time needed in the debriefing for explanations, comparisons and comments. The minimum number is probably eight and there is no maximum. It would be possible to run the event with six or seven participants, but in that case the Final value fix (requiring four players to agree) can be dropped.

Resources

* Briefing sheet – one copy for each player.
* Value fixing rules – one copy for each player.
* Values chart – one for each player.
* Bank values chart – one for the Bank and perhaps enlarged on a chart or display board.
* Interim value fix form – to be held by the Bank – about one copy for every four players.
* Final value fix form – to be held by the Bank – about one copy for every eight players.
* Symbol cards – one set of five different symbols for each player.
* Scrap paper.
* Self-assessment sheet – one copy for each participant (see suggestions in **Debriefing** section).

Method

1 Before the game begins, cut out the Symbol cards and keep them in sets of five.

2 Arrange for some area where the Bank person (probably yourself) can display the Bank values chart, perhaps using a large display board or flip chart. The Bank is simply a publicity point for value fixes and, apart from checking that the value fix is legal according to the rules, it has no other function. However, it is important to note that the Bank must not verbally announce any value fixes, but simply write them on a board or chart.

3 Hand out the Briefing sheets, plus the Value fixing rules.

4 Hand out one complete set of Symbol cards (five different cards) and one copy of the Values chart to each player.

5 Show the players the Interim and Final value fix forms and tell them that they are available at the Bank if required.

6 Set a time limit for the completion of the game.

7 Do not allow trading to commence until each player has filled in their personal values on their Values chart. Check that this has been done correctly.

Debriefing

This is one of the Five simple events listed in the Introduction and the easiest way to debrief a simple event is to ask the participants to fill in the Self-assessment sheets individually and use the results as a basis for discussion. The alternative is to take a more flexible approach and tailor the debriefing according to the particular course, the type of participants and significant episodes that occurred during the action. The following questions and suggestions could be used as a guide not only for the debriefing but also as a check-list of the sorts of things you could watch for in the action itself. (See also **Running the debriefing**, Introduction.)

It could be a good idea for players to first remain in their final pairs, work out and check their scores and exchange ideas about diplomacy, negotiation, planning and problem solving.

Apart from determining the 'winner' (which is of minor importance), the joint discussion could concentrate on the points reported by the pairs from their mini-debriefing.

Were there any interesting strategies? For example, did anyone discuss not only what value fixes to request, but when to make the request? Were there any secret deals in which four people decided on a final fix and delayed making it until the last minute? Although bargaining had to be on a one-to-one basis, did players realize that they were not limited to one exchange with another player but could, for example, exchange a heart for a tick and a star for an arrow?

The most interesting evidence could be the revelations of the thoughts of the players regarding negotiation, diplomacy and problem solving. Did players find it more diplomatic (and quicker) to reveal their Values charts rather than conceal them?

Did any patterns emerge regarding the personal value fixing – for example, did a majority prefer hearts to stars or the other way round? Did anyone try to gain a trading advantage by fixing their preferences in the opposite order to what they imagined other players would choose?

Did players show diplomacy? Were they polite, subtle, imaginative, open, humorous, friendly, energetic?

This is a game that starts with each player ranking five symbols (arrow, diamond, heart, star and tick) in order of personal value. Players meet in pairs and Symbol cards are traded on a one-for-one basis. The official value of individual symbols can be fixed by agreement.

The first stage is for each player to fix their own personal values for the five Symbol cards. The five values are five, four, three, two, one, with five being the highest value and one the lowest. For example if a player gives the star the value of two and the arrow the value of four, then for that player the arrow is twice as valuable as the star. Thus, each player starts with five different values for the symbols, which must add up to 15. At the end of the game, the highest possible score is 25 (5 cards, each worth 5) and the lowest score is 5 (5 cards, each worth 1).

All players must fill in their personal fix on their Values chart before any trading can begin. Show your personal fix to the facilitator. You do not have to reveal your personal fix to other players.

All trading must be in pairs, never in threes or more. You can meet the same person twice.

Although the Bank will publish all value fixes (by writing them on a board or chart) the fixes will not be announced verbally, so you may find it useful to keep an eye on the Bank values chart and enter any value fixes on your own Values chart to keep it up to date.

Value fixing rules

If you wish to fix a value, go to the Bank and obtain either the Interim value fix form or the Final value fix form.

To fix an interim value for a symbol you need the agreement of only one other player who must also sign the Interim value fix form. An interim value fix has priority over all personal value fixes for that particular symbol. It will probably mean that some players will have two symbols at the same value, For example, if a player has a personal value of five for an arrow and two for a star and the value of a star is given an interim value fix of five, then, for that player, both star and arrow are worth five at that stage. The same can happen in reverse if the value fixed is low rather than high.

A final value fix has priority over both personal value fixes and interim value fixes for that particular symbol and operates in the same way as an interim value fix, except that it needs the signatures of four players, not two. This means that the person with a Final value fix form must have separate meetings with at least three other players before the form is completed because it is forbidden for more than two players to meet together.

For the Bank to agree to fix the values, the following conditions must obtain in both the interim category of fix and the final category of fix:

1 the symbol must not already have an official value in that category of fix
2 the value must not be the same as one already allocated in that category of fix
3 none of the signatories must have already participated in a value fix in that category.

These rules mean that any player can participate in only two value fixes (one interim and one final) during the game. The rules also mean that a final fix can be made even though there has been no interim fix for that symbol.

Values chart

Symbol	Personal fix	Bank value: interim fix	Bank value: final fix	Final value
➤				
◆				
♥				
★				
✔				
Total	**15**			

Bank values chart

Symbols	Interim values fix	Final values fix
➤		
◆		
♥		
★		
✔		

Interim value fix form

Symbol ....   *Value* ....

Signed by   *(a)* ....   *(b)* ....

Interim value fix form

Symbol ....   *Value* ....

Signed by   *(a)* ....   *(b)* ....

Interim value fix form

Symbol ....   *Value* ....

Signed by   *(a)* ....   *(b)* ....

Interim value fix form

Symbol ....   *Value* ....

Signed by   *(a)* ....   *(b)* ....

Interim value fix form

Symbol ....   *Value* ....

Signed by   *(a)* ....   *(b)* ....

Final value fix form

Symbol .... Value ....

Signed by (a) .... (b) ....

Signed by (c) .... (d) ....

Final value fix form

Symbol .... Value ....

Signed by (a) .... (b) ....

Signed by (c) .... (d) ....

Final value fix form

Symbol .... Value ....

Signed by (a) .... (b) ....

Signed by (c) .... (d) ....

Final value fix form

Symbol .... Value ....

Signed by (a) .... (b) ....

Signed by (c) .... (d) ....

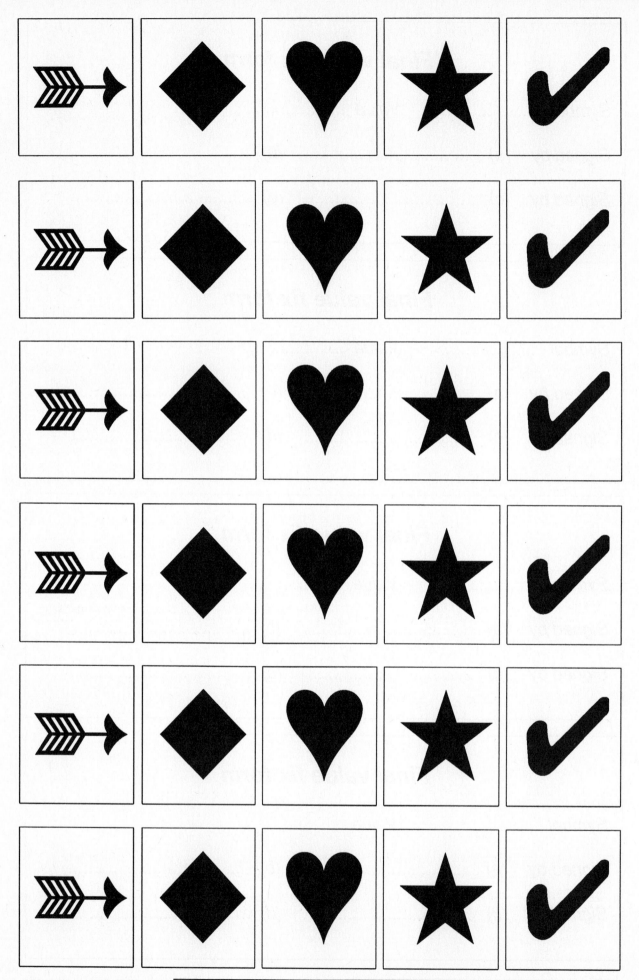

How did you begin? For example, did you start by working out a strategy for the game – perhaps by trying to gain a trading advantage by fixing your own preferences in the opposite order to what you imagined most other players would choose?

What was your negotiating style – were you friendly, open, suspicious, energetic, subtle?

If you reached agreement on an interim or final value fix did you consider the timing of it, perhaps delaying it?

How did you handle disagreements?

How do you assess yourself?

Skills	Poor	Fair	Good	Excellent
Efficiency				
Diplomacy				
Negotiation				
Planning				
Problem solving				
(Other)				

How do you assess the other players?

Skills	Poor	Fair	Good	Excellent
Efficiency				
Diplomacy				
Negotiation				
Planning				
Problem solving				
(Other)				

40 *Women managers*

Description

This is a simulation set in the Republic of Delta about the Executors of a large trust seeking to promote, enhance and improve the status of women in business and management.

Objectives

To enhance the skills of communication, planning, presentation and team building in a context involving gender.

Time and numbers

With small numbers allow about an hour and, for large numbers, up to two hours. The minimum number is six – two pairs as promotional agencies Alpha and Beta and two participants as Executors of the Trust. With 20 participants, it could either be run as one event with 4 participants as Executors of the Trust and 8 each as the Alpha and Beta agencies, or it could be run as 2 parallel events with 10 in each event. There is no maximum number.

Resources

* Briefing sheet – one copy for each participant.
* Organization identity tags – one tag for each group.
* Letter from the Trust – one copy for each participant.
* Scrap paper.

Method

1 Hand out the Briefing sheets, perhaps marking them to divide the participants into the Alpha and Beta Promotional Agencies and Executors of the Trust.

2 Retrieve the Briefing sheets and hand out the Organization identity tags, plus the copies of the Letter from the Trust, plus scrap paper.

3 Discuss the facilities for the presentation. Preferably a special area should be arranged, which might mean rearranging the furniture during the event.

4 Set a deadline for the start of the debriefing.

5 If you are at any time asked a question involving ethics, perhaps a whispered 'Are we allowed to offer a bribe to one of the trustees?', the best answer is probably something along the lines of 'I am not in this event' or 'I am invisible'. However, if the questioner is not familiar with the methodology, then you could explain that a simulation is not a game with fixed rules, it is like real life, actions are voluntary but consequences follow.

Debriefing

It could be useful to start with each team revealing any hidden thoughts or strategies. For example, was any attempt made by the Beta and Gamma groups to collaborate, perhaps each concentrating on one aspect, hoping that the contract could be divided between them? Did anyone offer a bribe and what was the result?

Within each group did everyone behave professionally or did some people remain in their personal mode and argue for or against feminism? Did each team work together as a team? Was anyone selected to take overall charge and coordinate the planning activities? Was the work divided up or was it all done by a committee?

Did anyone suggest having a brainstorming session? Did the promotional agencies submit anything in writing to the Trust? Did they envisage this option? Did they produce any visual aids for use in their presentation? Were the presentations team efforts or did one person stand up and give a lecture?

Note: Another simulation involving gender in Delta is event 36, Gender in law.

This is a simulation in the Republic of Delta about the Executors of a large trust seeking to improve the status of women in business and management.

George Gamma, the international property magnate, died last year, leaving a Trust fund of ten million pounds to 'promote, enhance and improve the status of women in business and management'. The Executors of the George Gamma Trust circulated an invitation to organizations to produce a plan for the spending of the money. The Trust has narrowed down the applicants to two: Alpha Promotions and Beta Promotions.

You will be Executives working for Alpha Promotions or Beta Promotions or Executors of the Trust. You will have a letter from the Trust to Alpha and Beta concerning presentations to be made. The Trust is in charge of the timing, order and facilities for the presentations. Executors of the Trust can visit the agencies from time to time to discuss arrangements. It is up to the Trust to decide whether to announce its decisions immediately after the presentations or whether to defer a decision for a few days to allow time for more considered appraisal.

There are no rules about informal contacts between Alpha and Beta, although neither side would formally sit round the table with the other.

What the Letter from the Trust does not explain is that Delta is a country with no specific legislation for equal opportunities and human rights, apart from general provisions regarding equality before the law and the concept of fair dealings. Deltan society is traditionally male orientated. Until 50 years ago, women did not have the right to vote. Until five years ago, women were not allowed to sit on juries.

There is no law to stop women being Prime Ministers, but Delta has never had a female in that office. Only one woman has ever been a minister, which was in the last government in the post of Minister for the Arts. Of 200 Members of Parliament, only 11 are women. Of the 100 top companies, none has a woman as managing director. There is no law to stop women being appointed customs officers, but all are men. There are no women among senior staff of Deltan Intelligence and the Head of Intelligence has always been male. By tradition, no woman is employed to do a dirty job – drainage workers, miners, soldiers, waste collectors are all men. Women in business in Delta are highly regarded as secretaries and typists and are treated with great respect and courtesy by men and there are few cases of sexual harassment.

George Gamma Trust

Alpha Promotions

Beta Promotions

George Gamma Trust

To: Alpha Promotions
           Beta Promotions

We have reached the final stages of the selection procedure and your two promotion companies are now the only contenders for the contract.

We now wish you to make a personal presentation, setting out the main thrust of your proposed campaigns and giving a few concrete examples of how you would seek to carry out the task. We shall be looking for imaginative ideas.

We shall be available for consultation regarding the facilities and will be pleased to answer any queries you might have. While you are preparing for the presentations, we shall be informing you of the time limits, the order in which you make the presentations and any other matters.

We will allow each agency to watch the presentation given by the other. Naturally, we will be displeased if the presentations are not watched in respectful silence. We will question each agency after their presentation and it is possible that we will allow the other agency to ask questions also. We will discuss this option with you before the presentations.

We do not rule out the possibility that the contract might be split between your two agencies. After your presentations we may be in a position to announce an immediate decision, but it is more likely that we shall need several days for careful discussion before announcing a result.

Personal areas

41 *Assortment of clerks*

Description

This is a simulation about a large organization that has to make cuts in clerical staff because of the introduction of a computer system. Clerical staff with computer experience are already being kept on as computer operators and there are no further vacancies. The other Clerks are to be interviewed. Some will stay on as Clerks and some will be made redundant.

The hidden agenda is that Interviewers are required to approve the performance of a Clerk at the first interview and sack a Clerk during the second interview. Do not run this event unless you feel confident that in the debriefing you can cope with anyone who is upset at being sacked or upset at having to terminate a person's contract.

Objectives

To enhance the skills of communication and counselling.

Time and numbers

With small numbers, the event would last about half an hour. With larger numbers more time will be required in the debriefing for explanation, comparison and comment and the event could last between an hour and an hour and a half. The minimum number is four – two Clerks and two Interviewers. There is no maximum number.

Resources

* Briefing sheet – one copy for each participant.
* Interviewers' instructions – one copy for each Interviewer.
* Clerks' information sheet – one copy for each Clerk.
* Forms A and B – one copy for each Clerk.
* Scrap paper.

Method

1 Mark the Briefing sheets to divide the participants at random into two equal groups of individuals – Clerks and Interviewers. Arrange the furniture for the interviews, perhaps having tables around the walls of the room so that the Clerks can move for the second interviews in a clockwise direction. Have ample space between the tables. Set a time limit for the two interviews. Explain that for the second interview the Clerks should move to the next Interviewer on the right.

2 Retrieve the Briefing sheets. Hand out the Interviewers' instructions – one copy to each of the Interviewers. Hand out the Clerks' information sheet – one copy for each Clerk. Hand out copies of Forms A and B to the Clerks. Make available the scrap paper.

3 In order to preserve the secrecy of the hidden agenda, it is important that the Interviewers should not see the Clerks' information sheets, so retrieve these sheets after the Clerks have filled in Forms A and B but before they go for their first interview.

4 Before the start of the first interview it may be a good idea to emphasize that Clerks should keep Form B concealed as it relates to a different Clerk role in a different department. This advice will also help to preserve the hidden agenda and not confuse the Interviewers during the first interview if they accidentally see the answers on Form B as well as Form A.

5 Make sure that all the first interviews stop promptly at the time limit and that all the Clerks go to a different Interviewer for the second interview.

Debriefing   Start by disclosing the hidden agenda – the Interviewers' instructions and the Clerks' information sheet. You can, if you wish, explain that the second option for the Interviewers was to increase plausibility. (If this second option was used, then a Clerk must have filled in one of the forms incorrectly.) The reasons for having three favourable qualities in the answer on Form A and one unfavourable quality in the answer on Form B were (a) to put ideas into the minds of the Interviewers that they were forbidden to discuss – not an altogether unusual situation in business – and (b) to provide evidence for a potential discussion in the debriefing about the extent to which desirable and undesirable qualities in a particular job may depend upon the actual department (and/or organization) in which the job is done.

The central aspect was probably the termination of contracts. Were Clerks shattered by being made redundant? Did anyone lose their temper? How positive was their reaction – did they look backwards or forwards? Did any Clerk decide to appeal against being made redundant? Did any Clerk ask for counselling?

How did the Interviewers break the bad news? Did they tell the Clerks that their work was unsatisfactory? Did both Clerks and Interviewers accept the word 'redundancy' as a polite code for easing the pain of dismissal with neither side wishing to explore why one Clerk had been made 'redundant' while another Clerk was kept on? Did any Interviewer recommend counselling or recommend that a Clerk should appeal?

This is a simulation about a large organization that has to make cuts in clerical staff because of the introduction of a computer system. Clerical staff with computer experience are already being kept on as computer operators and there are no further vacancies. The other Clerks are to be interviewed. Some will stay on as Clerks and some will be made redundant. You are either a member of the clerical staff or an Interviewer.

Each participant will be involved in two interviews. There are six departments – Administration, Finance, Production, Publicity, Research and Sales – and Clerks must choose which department they are working in. Clerks must write this department on Form A, which they must hand to the first Interviewer. For the second interview they take on the role of a different Clerk and must choose a different department and enter their choice on Form B. If you are a Clerk and if you fill in Form B before the first interview you must keep it concealed because it relates to the second interview only.

The second interview must be with a different Interviewer.

On Forms A and B the third question relates to research, but the research answers themselves must not be discussed during the interviews. At the end of each interview, the Interviewer should hand the form to the facilitator and the research answers could be discussed during the debriefing in relation to job qualities and departments.

Outside the interviews, everyone must operate individually, not as a group.

Do not playact. Behave professionally.

Interviewers' instructions

At your first interview, the clerical worker should give you Form A only, and in the second interview Form B only. On both forms the Clerks give their first name and the department they work in. Thank them for filling in the form. If they refer to the Research answer, then say that it will be used for research purposes only. Do not discuss the actual words they have written.

However, the number of words in the Research answer is a confidential code as follows:

* three words shows that their work has been very satisfactory and that they will be kept on as Clerks; you should discuss how they are finding their work in their department
* two words shows that their work has been marginally satisfactory and you must issue a warning about the possibility of redundancy; you should discuss how they are finding their work in their department
* one word shows that their work has been unsatisfactory and you must tell them that they have been made redundant.

You must not reveal that there is a confidential code.

Note: Although termination of employment may be difficult, you should concentrate on helping the person take a positive attitude and to look towards the future not back to the past. Ask them about their plans.

You are permitted to point out that counselling services will be provided if required. You can say that they will receive a generous severance settlement based on length of service and salary (do not go into details). You can say that many Clerks are being made redundant (do not use the words 'sacked' or 'dismissed') and that they have the right of appeal against redundancy should they wish to go through the procedures.

Clerks' information

Form A is for the first interview only and Form B for the second interview only. Hand over the appropriate form at the start of each interview.

Each form requires three answers.

1 Name Both forms ask you to fill in your name. Give your first name only.

2 Department When filling in Form A, choose one of the six departments you think you would be comfortable working for from Administration, Finance, Production, Publicity, Research, Sales. For the second interview, you take the role of a Clerk in a different department, so write in your second choice of department on Form B.

3 Research answers On Form A, write down the following three qualities in the order in which you think they are desirable in clerks working for your particular department:

* reliability
* accuracy
* speed.

You must write all **three** words, not just one or two. (Don't know or other variants are not allowed.)

On Form B write down which of the following two qualities you think is the most undesirable in clerical staff in the second department you are now working in:

* dishonesty
* unreliability.

Write **one** word only, not both words or neither. (Don't know or other variants are not allowed.)

The interviews

The interviews will concentrate entirely on your personal situation in relation to the department in which you work. The Interviewers have been instructed not to discuss your Research answers. It may be a good idea to work out in advance how you will cope with the situation should you be made redundant.

Form A   *First interview*

Name: _____

Department: _____

Research answer: _____

Form B   *Second interview*

Name: _____

Department: _____

Research answer: _____

Form A   *First interview*

Name: _____

Department: _____

Research answer: _____

Form B   *Second interview*

Name: _____

Department: _____

Research answer: _____

42 *Born today*

Description Babies with at least 70 years of life expectancy meet professional Trainers and Counsellors. The event can be run in the format of an icebreaker.

Objectives To enhance the skills of counselling, planning and team building.

Time and numbers With small numbers, it would take about half an hour. With larger numbers more time will be required in the debriefing for explanations, comparisons and comments so the event could last between an hour and an hour and a half. The minimum number is four – two Babies, one Trainer and one Counsellor. There is no maximum number. You can choose between running it as an icebreaker, with as many participants meeting each other as possible, or having fewer interviews of greater depth.

Resources
* Briefing sheet – one copy for each participant.
* Expectations sheet – one copy for each Baby.
* Training sheet – one copy for each Trainer.
* Counselling sheet – one copy for each Counsellor.
* Identification tags – one (of three) for each participant.

Method
1 Discuss the timing. For example, if you want to run it in the format of an icebreaker it may be useful to fix time limits for individual meetings and possibly have everyone change partners at the same time.

2 Hand out the Briefing sheets – one for each participant – perhaps marking the sheets to determine who has which role. About half the participants should have the role of Babies and the other half should be equally divided between Counsellors and Trainers and, with large numbers, it could be a good idea to have an Observer or two.

3 Retrieve the Briefings sheets and hand out the Identification tags, together with the appropriate Expectation, Training and Counselling sheets.

Debriefing It could be useful to have mini-debriefings of the three groups separately – Babies, Trainers and Counsellors. The subsequent joint session could begin with the three groups reporting their findings.

How useful did the Babies find the Trainers and Counsellors in planning their lives? Did the professionals find the Babies cooperative and imbued with team building? What happened when Counsellors met Trainers? What occurred when Babies met Babies, Trainers met Trainers and Counsellors met Counsellors?

Were confidences respected? Did the professionals pass on professional tips to each other? Were Counsellors more frank with their colleagues than with Trainers and vice versa?

How did the event work as an icebreaker? Were the discussions helpful in getting to know people? Were people polite, friendly, brusque, pompous, sympathetic, self-centred, imaginative?

Babies with at least 70 years of life expectancy meet professional Trainers and Counsellors. Everyone must meet in pairs, not in threes or more.

Babies are babies only in age and have full powers of mature thought, language and experience when they meet people. In a sense they are professional babies. All Babies will receive an Expectations sheet of 70 years expectancy that can be marked with their own expectations plus advice from Counsellors and training relating to particular decades. Before the first meeting, Babies should fill in at least one but no more than three expectancy milestones. Possible milestones include marriage, divorce and retirement. Death cannot be entered because the life expectancy is greater than the 70 years on the Expectations sheet. The Babies can change their life expectations milestones as a result of their discussions.

When Trainers and Counsellors meet Babies it is their duty to offer advice, information and behave as a member of a team to enhance the quality of life of the Babies. Trainers will probably concentrate on careers and Counsellors will probably concentrate on personal issues, although there is no rigid demarcation line.

When professionals meet each other they can discuss the Babies from a professional standpoint, perhaps without revealing names. Similarly, when Babies meet Babies they can have a professional discussion about the quality and helpfulness of their advisers.

Both Trainers and Counsellors will have a sheet on which to record meetings and comments.

Expectations sheet

Years	Milestones	Comments
0 to 10		
10 to 20		
20 to 30		
30 to 40		
40 to 50		
50 to 60		
60 to 70		

Training sheet

Name: ....

I met...	Comments

Counselling sheet

Name: ....

I met...	Comments

Baby	**Trainer**	**Counsellor**
Name:	Name:	Name: ....
Baby	**Trainer**	**Counsellor**
Name:	Name:	Name: ....
Baby	**Trainer**	**Counsellor**
Name:	Name:	Name: ....
Baby	**Trainer**	**Counsellor**
Name:	Name:	Name: ....

43 *Doppelgangers and mirrors*

Description

This is a simulation set in the Misty World of Identity. The participants meet in pairs. Imaginary people facing some problem of identity meet professional advisers, either Doppelgangers or Mirrors. Participants change roles.

Objectives

To enhance the skills of communication, counselling and planning.

Time and numbers

With small numbers, the event would take about half an hour to an hour. With larger numbers more time will be required in the debriefing for explanations, comparisons and comments and the event could last between one and two hours. The minimum number is four – with two Doppelgangers and two Mirrors. There is no maximum number.

Resources

* Briefing sheet – one copy for each participant.
* Personal identity chart – one copy for each participant.
* Doppelganger sheet – one copy for each Doppelganger (half the participants).
* Mirror sheet – one copy for each Mirror (the other half of the participants).
* Ritual object – one for every two participants (these should be identical objects and can be any object that is convenient and easy to hold – cups, spoons, rulers, tape recorders).

Method

1 It could be useful to set a time limit for each meeting, perhaps giving a signal for people to change partners. If, however, the main aim is to enhance the skills of communication, counselling and planning, the length of each meeting could be left to the discretion of the participants, perhaps asking them not to prolong meetings if other participants are waiting.

2 Hand out the Briefing sheets – one for each participant. Arrange the space and furniture so that pairs can be as widely separated as possible and meet in reasonable privacy. Discuss the time factor.

3 Hand out at random the Doppelganger sheets to half the participants and the Mirror sheets to the other half. Hand out a Personal identity chart, to everyone. Retrieve the Briefing sheets.

4 At random, hand out to half the participants the Ritual objects – which identifies them as the Imaginary people. Perhaps you could remind them what it says in the Briefing sheet, that they do not change roles within meetings, but that, at the end of a meeting, they should toss a coin (or decide among themselves) whether to pass on the Ritual object or not.

Note: Although most participants will gain personally from this event because of the high level of empathy and sympathy, there is the possibility that someone, despite the instructions, will spill out their own personal troubles and become upset. Be cautious about running the event if you do not know the participants well. If anyone shows signs of becoming distressed, then you could suggest that they take the role of a Helper or Observer. Note also, however, that the event has built-in cushions to prevent people being hurt, namely hypothetical cases related to work situations (not personal life) and frequent changes of role.

Debriefing

It is probably a good idea for participants to start by having a mini-debriefing in two groups – Doppelgangers and Mirrors – and discuss the professional aspects of the experience.

One line of inquiry in the subsequent discussion could be whether people learned from the early meetings how to make their professional roles more effective. Did they become better Doppelgangers or Mirrors? How sympathetic and intuitive were the Doppelgangers? How observant, imaginative and helpful were the Mirrors?

As for the Imaginary people, did they vary the role personality between meetings or simply build up on the personality they invented at the start? How many people changed their real sex or age or race? Were imaginative details plausible? If they were implausible or extreme, were they valuable in providing clear examples?

How friendly were the participants? Were the brief discussions shallow, superficial, businesslike, friendly, sympathetic, reassuring, helpful?

Briefing 43 Doppelgangers and mirrors

This is a simulation set in the Misty World of Identity. Participants meet in pairs in which one is the Imaginary person seeking advice about a problem of identity related to work and the other is a professional adviser – either a Doppelganger or Mirror.

Everyone has two roles – the Imaginary person and either the Doppelganger or the Mirror. Everyone meets privately in pairs, changing roles between meetings but not during meetings.

The Imaginary person should begin by inventing details that might fit an imaginary problem of identity, which must be related to work, not simply a personal problem. For example, 'My age is A, my sex is B and I feel insecure at work because I cannot seem to express the real me'. All these statements could be completely imaginary, most should be imaginary and some must be imaginary. You must never be your own real self, although you can be similar if you wish. Try to be a different Imaginary person at least twice during the event.

Playacting and anguish should be avoided. Simply outline the facts relating to the identity problem unemotionally, as if it were a case study seen from the inside.

To think yourself into being a Doppelganger or Mirror will probably be more difficult than your Imaginary person role, but it will become easier, particularly when you find out how other professionals advise you when you are the Imaginary person. Doppelgangers tend to be sympathetic and subjective; Mirrors tend to be practical and objective.

Imaginary people must hold a Ritual object and must not meet other Imaginary people. Similarly, professional people must not meet each other. At the end of each meeting, toss a coin or reach agreement about whether to pass on the Ritual object and thereby change roles for the next meeting. Do not try to stick to the same role for the whole of the event.

After each meeting, you can record on the appropriate form the name of the person you met and jot down anything that seemed interesting, unusual, significant, etc. The Personal identity charts are to help the Imaginary people find their way through the mist of doubts and uncertainties while the Doppelganger and Mirror sheets are more businesslike.

Personal identity chart

Name: _____

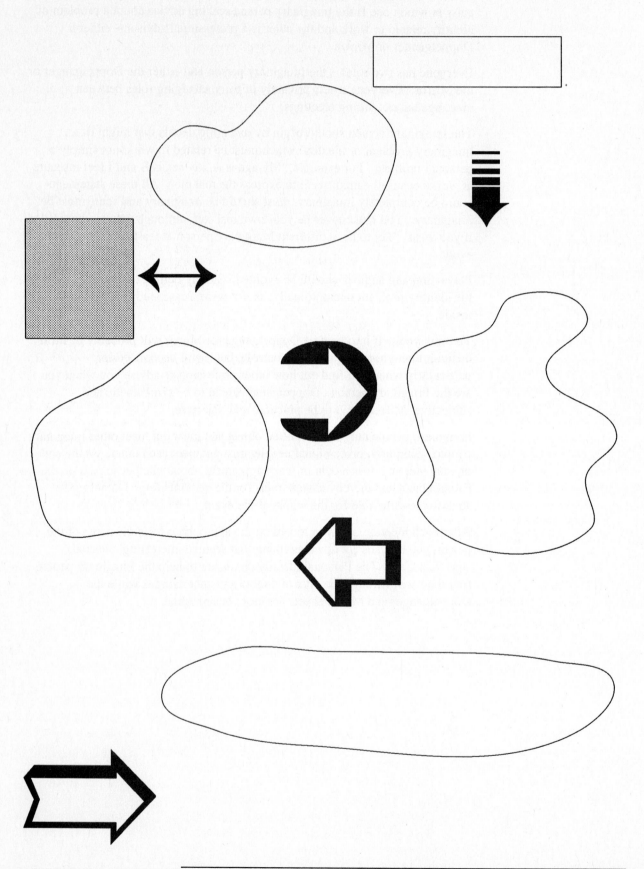

Name: _____

First words on meeting an Imaginary person should be as follows.

I am your Doppelganger.
We are identical, the same.
I live in a parallel world and I know how you feel.
I can give you advice about yourself.

I met...	Comments

Mirror

Name: _____

First words on meeting an Imaginary person should be as follows.

I am a Mirror.
I can show you how you appear to the world.
I can give you advice about your image.

I met...	Comments

44 *Health machine*

Description This is a simulation in which Managers of Centrum Hospital of the Republic of Alpha discuss what to do with an interplanetary health machine.

Objectives To enhance the skills of diplomacy, negotiation and planning.

Time and numbers Running it as one event would take about half an hour. With several groups allow an hour or more because of the opportunities in the debriefing for explanations, comparisons and comments. The ideal number is four. The minimum number is three, in which case Opinion D could be given to someone as a second opinion. There is no maximum number.

Resources
* Briefing sheet – one copy for each participant.
* Message from Donator – one copy for each participant.
* Opinion tags – set of four to each group.
* Hospital notepaper – to be made available as required.
* Scrap paper – to be made available.

Method

1 Before running the event, consider the possibility of having real refreshments for the refreshment sessions. Another plausible item could be a token health machine (a box or even a laptop computer) that would have the advantage of focusing attention on the issue. A possible disadvantage is that if participants are not used to simulations, someone might treat the token machine as an object of fun.

2 If you are running more than one event, divide the participants into groups of four at random, perhaps by marking the Briefing sheets, laying them face down and allowing participants to pick their own. With five participants, one participant could be an Observer or share an Opinion tag. With six or more, the simulation could be run as separate events. Discuss time limits, refreshment breaks and locations of meetings.

3 Give each group a set of the four Opinion tags, placed face down, letting participants pick their own. Retrieve all the Briefing sheets. Hand out Hospital notepaper and scrap paper.

4 Start the simulation with people standing up and meeting privately in pairs, not as a committee.

Debriefing If there were parallel events, it could be a good idea to allow each group to debrief themselves.

A joint debriefing session could begin with each group taking it in turns to explain what happened. As the issues themselves will have been explored during the simulation, the debriefing can consider the skills of diplomacy and planning.

How effective was the diplomacy? Did anyone look for allies? How successful was the argument for rotation of priorities (in scarce resource situations in real life the priorities are often applied haphazardly on a case-by-case basis, sometimes one criteria having priority, sometimes another)?

As no other person knew about the machine, did their planning include considering the options of secrecy or publicity? Did they make arrangements to place the machine in a safe place or to give a news conference or to hold talks with the Government? Did they decide to seek anyone's advice? Did they make any formal statement? Did they use the Hospital notepaper?

What options were explored? Did anyone consider the national and international implications? Although the machine had to remain at the Hospital did they a consider selling or donating the right to choose the patients? Did they consider treating nationals of foreign countries? Did they consider granting the right of choice of patients to the United Nations?

This is a simulation in which Managers of Centrum Hospital of the Republic of Alpha discuss what to do with an interplanetary health machine.

Centrum Hospital in Alpha is run as a charity and takes both National Health and private patients. It is not controlled by the Government.

You are all Managers who are in charge of hospital policy. You arrive at the Boardroom for a meeting and discover that a small health machine has been beamed down onto the table by Donator, a charity spaceship, together with copies of an explanatory message. No other person knows what has occurred.

The health machine is slightly larger than a laptop computer. At the rear of the machine are two buttons marked 'Start' and 'Stop'. You will each have the text of the Message from the interplanetary charity ship..

When the meeting begins, there are four different views about which patients should receive priority. You will receive an Opinion tag that you must state at the start of the meeting. After that you can change your mind and adopt someone else's opinion or think up a priority scale of your own. You can also discuss, decide and plan any action whatsoever regarding the health machine.

Your normal meetings are usually routine affairs and no one takes the chair, but this meeting may be different. Hospital notepaper and scrap paper will be available.

Before the meeting begins there is a refreshments period when you should stand up, meditate on the problem and try to meet all your colleagues individually. There will be a similar refreshment break halfway through the meeting. During the refreshment breaks, do not all meet together as a group.

Donator

Interplanetary charity ship

We, of the interplanetary charity ship Donator, do hereby give to Centrum Hospital a health machine, to be under the control of you, the Managers of the Hospital. We do so because Alpha is an average country in terms of wealth, freedom and democracy. Not only will the sick benefit from the machine but it will also be educational for you to determine who should be allowed to use it.

The health machine will cure any patient of any disease whatsoever, but it cannot mend broken bones, heal wounds or halt the natural process of ageing.

It can treat only one patient at a time and each patient requires 24 hours for the treatment to be completed. Patients do not need to remain close to the machine throughout that time. All that is required is for the patient to lightly touch the front surface of the machine with their fingertips at the beginning and at the end of the period. The health machine needs no operative skill. Simply press the Start button to start the machine and the Stop button to stop the machine.

Warning:

1 If removed from Centrum Hospital the machine will cease to operate.
2 The machine cannot be copied — it will automatically destroy itself if opened.

Good luck and goodbye.

Opinion A

Priority should be given to those people most in need – a decision to be taken by doctors.

Opinion B

Priority should be given to young people.

Opinion C

Priority should be given to important and famous people.

Opinion D

Priorities should rotate, first applying one criteria then another.

Centrum Hospital
Alpha

45 *Management philosophy*

Description

This is a simulation involving a country where employers have been divided into different groups according to their managerial philosophy. Counsellors interview Job seekers to see if their philosophies are compatible with those of a potential employer. The simulation could be run in the format of an icebreaker.

Objectives

To enhance the skills of communication and counselling.

Time and numbers

With small numbers, the event would probably last for about half an hour. With larger numbers, allow about an hour to an hour and a half because of the extra time needed in the debriefing for explanations, comparisons and discussion. The minimum number is probably four. There is no maximum number.

Resources

* Briefing sheet – one copy for each participant.
* Interview sheet – one copy for each participant.
* Scrap paper.

Method

1 Decide whether to use the event mainly as an icebreaker and have a relatively large number of meetings or whether to concentrate on counselling and have fewer meetings. For an icebreaker, you could set a time limit for each meeting, perhaps giving a signal to change partners.

2 Consider the furniture arrangements. If you have a table and two chairs for each meeting, you should locate them so that the interviews are as far apart as possible.

3 Hand out the Briefing sheets – one copy for each participant and discuss the timing.

4 Hand out the Interview sheets – one for each participant. Retrieve the Briefing sheets. Make scrap paper available.

Debriefing

If there were more than about eight participants it could be a good idea for people to remain in their final pairs and debrief themselves before the joint session. The general discussion could begin with people taking it in turns to disclose anything that was interesting, significant, helpful or surprising.

How well did the pairs communicate? Did they stick to philosophical issues or delve into personalities? Were the Counsellors sympathetic, friendly, helpful? Were the Job seekers specific? Were counselling skills employed or did the Counsellors behave like information clerks?

A key issue is that people are often self-contradictory, saying that they want one thing but really wanting another. Did this issue come out? How was it dealt with? If the discussion deals with individual participants' personal problems, it should be made clear that these cases are hypothetical (even if they are close to the truth). The advantage of hypothetical cases is that people can express their opinions more readily.

This is a simulation involving a country where employers have been divided into different groups according to their managerial philosophy. Counsellors interview Job seekers to see if their philosophies are compatible with those of a potential employer.

You have the roles of both Counsellors and Job seekers. You meet in pairs and first decide who should be the Counsellor. Halfway through each meeting, you change roles – the Counsellor becoming the Job seeker and vice versa.

The three categories of employer are:

1 Philosophy of Efficiency – the main criteria is whether it works well
2 Philosophy of Happiness – the happiness of workers is the prime concern
3 Philosophy of Equality – equality of opportunity is the chief factor in decision making.

The three categories are not necessarily incompatible, but the categories reflect the priority of values in a company. Before you begin the event, you should choose a category for yourself as Job seeker. You can change to another category during the event if you feel the need to do so. If the Job seeker mentions personal problems, these should be hypothetical and imaginary, not drawn from the participant's own life.

The Counsellors' job is:

* to try to find out if the Job seeker has chosen a category that is not too idealistic and which fits in with their normal behaviour (for example, some Job seekers might say they are in favour of happiness whereas, on questioning, it turns out that they are in favour of it only if it comes free of charge)
* to clarify the issues – to do this Counsellors can pose hypothetical questions, for example, 'How would you feel if the company's basic philosophy resulted in such-and-such?'
* to give whatever advice seems suitable.

Interview sheet

Name: _____

I met...	As a Counsellor I discussed...	As a Job seeker I discussed...

46 *Missing disc*

Description   A simulation in which the Security Manager of Workday Software interviews three other Managers, one of whom might have been responsible for the disappearance of a valuable confidential computer program.

Objectives   To enhance the skills of communication and diplomacy.

Time and numbers   With small numbers, the event will probably take about an hour. If there are several events run in parallel, more time will be needed in the debriefing for explanations, comparisons and comments and the event could then take up to two hours. The minimum is four – one for each role. There is no maximum number.

Resources
* Briefing sheet – one copy for each participant.
* Memo from Managing Director – one copy for each participant.
* Personal information sheets – a set of four sheets for each group.
* Report sheet – one copy for each participant.
* Scrap paper.

Method
1 Divide the participants at random into groups of four, perhaps by marking the Briefing sheets. If the numbers will not divide equally by four, you could make someone an Assistant Security Officer or an Observer.

2 The meeting is held in the Security Manager's office and there is a refreshment area where private talks can take place. Discuss timing and locations. If only limited space is available, the refreshment area could be anywhere that is reasonably private – a corridor, a garden or a far corner of the room.

3 Retrieve the Briefing sheets and hand out the copies of the Memo from the Managing Director and the Report sheet – one of each to each participant.

4 Allocate roles at random, perhaps by placing the four Personal information sheets face down and asking the participants to pick their own. Remind them about concealing these sheets.

5 Make scrap paper available.

Debriefing   If there were several parallel events, it could be a good idea to let each group debrief themselves. This could start with participants revealing their Personal information sheets and their Report sheets.

In the subsequent joint discussion, little time need be spent in speculating on who took the disc. It was not stolen by any of the three suspects. It can be assumed that it was not taken by the Security Manager otherwise this would be revealed in the Security Manager's Personal information sheet. (The Briefing sheet states that the true and relevant facts are revealed in the Personal information sheets.) Possibly a drawer was left unlocked and a secretary obtained access to the key of the safe and stole the disc. Perhaps the Managing Director either stole the disc or mislaid it somewhere.

The main issue is not what happened to the disc but how the participants behaved. Were they diplomatic? Did anyone make accusations? How well did they communicate, both in the private meetings and in the joint meetings?

Did any or all of the managers reveal details of what they knew about their colleagues? Did they exaggerate or even invent stories? (*Note*: Invented stories are not 'facts' in a simulation, they are invented stories and can be challenged as in real life.)

Did everyone behave with courtesy and consideration, thus respecting the wishes of the Managing Director who did not wish to disrupt the friendly atmosphere among the staff?

This is a simulation in which a Security Manager of Workday Software interviews three other Managers, one of whom might have been responsible for the disappearance of a valuable confidential computer program from a special safe designed to hold discs.

Workday Software is an independent company with a reputation for innovation. It is in the process of developing a revolutionary type of spreadsheet. The situation is explained in the Memo from the Managing Director. The true and relevant facts about your own position are given in your Personal Information sheet and you must not let any other participants see this. You must not invent 'facts' to win arguments, although you can make reasonable assumptions about the facts as given in your Personal information sheet and in the Memo from the Managing Director.

The Memo from the Managing Director requests that each manager should write a few sentences on the Report sheet, which will be treated with the utmost confidentiality. In the debriefing, of course, you will be expected to reveal hidden motives and confidential moves.

MEMO

From: Managing Director
To: Finance Manager, Research Manager, Sales Manager
Copy to: Security Manager

At 8.30 a.m. this morning I entered the Boardroom and placed in the safe the latest version of our new spreadsheet. When I went to collect the disc at noon it was not there.

I have no wish to do anything to disrupt the friendly cooperative behaviour of the staff. I would like the matter to be settled without fuss. Apart from my own key, the only other keys are held by the Managers of Finance, Research and Sales and I would like you to be interviewed as a group by the Security Manager in the Security Office.

Halfway through the meeting, you should take a break for coffee and snacks and the Security Manager can have a brief talk with each of you, privately and individually.

At the end of the meeting, I would be grateful if you would each, separately and privately, write a few lines for me on the Report sheet about the incident. I shall, of course, treat whatever you write with complete confidentiality.

Personal information: Security Manager

I have spoken to the secretaries of the three Managers. I have learned that at 9 a.m., the Finance Manager went into the Boardroom for about 10 minutes. At 10.15 a.m., the Research Manager went into the Boardroom for about half an hour. At about 11.20 a.m., the Sales Manager went into the Boardroom for about 2 minutes.

I know for a fact that the Finance Manager is now short of money, having made a disastrous investment on the Stock Exchange. It is common knowledge that the Research Manager is dissatisfied and may leave the company. I have learned that the Sales Manager has been betting on the horses and has run up a sizeable debt.

Personal information: Finance Manager

I entered the Boardroom at about 9 a.m. for 5 or 10 minutes. I opened the filing cabinet and looked at the previous balance sheet to see how it dealt with some sundry expenses. This was useful as I am at present engaged in drawing up the balance sheet for the current year. I did not open the safe and know nothing about the missing disc. I keep the key to the safe locked in my desk and only I have the key to my desk.

It is true that I made a disastrous investment on the Stock Exchange, but, although I am short of money, I am not in debt. It is common knowledge that the Research Manager is dissatisfied and may leave the company. I know that the Sales Manager has been betting on horses and has run up a sizeable debt.

Personal information: Research Manager

I was in the Boardroom for about half an hour sometime between 10 a.m. and 11 a.m. I looked in the filing cabinet for documents about the specifications for transfer systems between computers. I could have taken the documents back to my room, but it was quieter and easier to work in the Boardroom. I did not open the safe and know nothing about the missing disc. I keep the key to the safe locked in my desk and only I have the key to my desk.

It is true that I am dissatisfied with my job and may leave the company, as I feel I should be earning more money and having greater recognition for my ideas. I know that the Sales Manager has been betting on horses and has run up a sizeable debt. Another person with financial worries is the Finance Manager and it is common knowledge that he made a disastrous investment on the Stock Exchange.

Personal information: Sales Manager

I went to the Boardroom somewhere around 11.15 a.m. to look for the Exhibitions file. It was not in the filing cabinet so I went upstairs to the Advertising Department where I found it. I was in the Boardroom for no more than two or three minutes. I did not open the safe and know nothing about the missing disc. I keep the key to the safe locked in my desk and only I have the key to my desk.

It is true that I had been betting on horses and ran up a sizeable debt. However, I have now stopped gambling completely and I have already repaid most of the debt. I am not the only person with financial worries and I know that the Finance Manager has made a disastrous investment on the Stock Exchange. I also know that the Research Manager is dissatisfied and may leave the company.

47 *Prison prospects*

Description   This is a simulation about new Prisoners, Gang leaders and Senior warders. The job of the Prisoners is to convince the Gang leaders and Senior warders that they are speaking the truth and the job of the Gang leaders and Senior warders is to guess correctly whether this is true or false.

Objectives   To enhance the skills of communication and diplomacy.

Time and numbers   For small numbers, allow about half an hour for the event. The more participants there are, the greater will be the time needed in the debriefing for working out the results and for making explanations, comparisons and comments. With 20 participants the event could take up to an hour and a half. The minimum number is four – two new Prisoners, one Gang leader and one Senior warder – which means that each participant will meet three people. There is no maximum number.

Resources
* Briefing sheet – one copy for each participant.
* Individual progress sheet – one copy for each participant.
* Personal choice sheet – one copy for each new Prisoner.
* Gang leader's record sheet – one for each Gang leader.
* Senior warder's record sheet – one for each Senior warder.
* Results sheet – one copy for facilitator (or for Observer or Checker).
* Identity tags – enough to make half the participants new Prisoners, a quarter Senior warders and a quarter Gang leaders.

Method
1 With 20 or so participants it could be useful to have someone in the role of Observer or Checker who will handle the transferring of the entries on Personal choice sheets to the Results sheet.

2 Hand out the Briefing sheets and the Individual progress sheets – one of each to each participant.

3 Arrange the Identity tags so that half the participants will be new Prisoners and the other half more or less equally divided between Senior warders and Gang leaders. It is a good idea to place the tags face down and let participants pick their own.

4 Hand out the Personal choice sheets to new Prisoners, then hand out the Gang leader's record sheets to the Gang leaders and the Senior warder's record sheets to the Senior warders.

5 Retrieve the Personal choice sheets from the new Prisoners (making sure that they have been filled in correctly).

6 Retrieve the Briefing sheets and Individual progress sheets and announce the start of the meetings.

7 When the simulation has begun, sort out the Personal choice sheets into two groups according to their choice. This is to make it easier to work out the results. Enter the choices on the Results sheet.

8 At the end of the event, go through the Results sheet, one new Prisoner at a time, and ask the Senior warders and Gang leaders to give their assessments. Once the Results sheet has been filled in, the consequences

can be worked out. You have the option of either doing this personally on your own chart or using a display chart so that people can see what is happening and check the result. If you use a display chart, it might be more dramatic to enter the assessments of the Senior warders and Gang leaders before revealing each Prisoner's choice. Here follows an example of what a Results sheet might look like for six new Prisoners (Ada, Ben, Cal, Don, Eva and Fay), three Senior warders (Gus, Hal and Ina) and three Gang leaders (Joe, Kay and Len).

Prisoner's choice

Senior warders	Gang leaders	Assessed by Senior warders						Assessed by Gang leaders						Scores (no. of Ts)
		Gus	Hal	Ina				Joe	Kay	Len				
Ada		T 1	T 1	T 1				T 0	T 0	T 0				6
Ben		T 1	F 0	T 1				T 0	F 1	F 1				3
	Cal	F 1	T 0	F 1				T 1	T 1	T 1				4
	Don	F 1	T 0	F 1				T 1	T 1	T 1				4
	Eva	T 0	T 0	F 1				F 0	T 1	T 1				4
	Fay	T 0	F 1	F 1				F 0	F 0	T 1				2
		4	2	6				2	4	5				

Key: T = a guess that the statement of support is True
F = a guess that the statement of support is False

The effects of these results are as follows:

Prisoners:

Ada (6), with the highest score, ended up with an easy life for two years
Ben (3) stayed the same with an uneasy life for two years
Cal (4) Don (4) and Eva (4) stayed the same with an easy life for three years
Fay (2), with the lowest score, ended up with an uneasy life for three years

Senior warders:

Gus (4) remained a Senior warder
Hal (2) was demoted to Warder
Ina (6) was promoted to Chief warder

Gang leaders:

Joe (2) was demoted to an ordinary Prisoner
Kay (4) remained a Gang leader
Len (5) was promoted to Senior gang leader.

Debriefing

It could be useful to point out to the participants that they should not treat the scores too seriously as a 50 per cent score could be achieved by random guesswork. Perhaps the first step might be to divide them into their three groups and for each group have a mini-debriefing about professional aspects related to their group.

After the three groups have reported to the joint session, the discussion can be wideranging. It could cover any unusual or significant episodes and deal with the skills of communication and diplomacy.

Was there any consensus of personal choices among the Prisoners? What motivated their choices? How did they react to people in authority? When the Prisoners met each other, was there any conflict between self-interest and group loyalty? Did they freely pass on information about what they learned about the attitudes of individual Gang leaders and Senior warders.

Were there any differences in the attitudes of the Senior warders and Gang leaders to the new Prisoners? Did either tend to be more sympathetic? When Gang leaders met Senior warders was there hostility, fellow-feeling, mutual respect or even exchange of confidential information? When Senior warders met Senior warders and Gang leaders met Gang leaders, were they cooperative, honest, suspicious, deceitful?

How similar or dissimilar was the simulation to prison life or business life or life in any large institution?

Given the fact that meetings between new Prisoners and Senior warders/Gang leaders were loaded with suspicion were people generally polite, friendly, pompous, hostile, sympathetic, self-centred?

Note about ethics: Be prepared for the possibility that some participants may wish to discuss the negative effects of lying on both the liar and the person being lied to. If so, and if comparisons are being made with real life, it is worth pointing out that the simulation scenario is highly unusual.

1 Everyone knows in advance what the lie will be and that there is a 50–50 chance that it will occur when a prisoner meets a Senior warder or Gang leader.

2 The guesses made by the Senior warders and Gang leaders cover not only the false statements but also the true statements, so improvements in prison prospects depend on truth as well as falsehood.

If ethics becomes a major issue in the debriefing, perhaps the most interesting aspect would be the spontaneous and voluntary truths and falsehoods rather than the obligatory ones. The discussion could cover not only what happened between Prisoners and the Senior warders and Gang leaders but also the lies, deceits, frankness and disclosure of true or false information at meetings between colleagues and meetings between Senior warders and Gang leaders.

This is a simulation about new Prisoners, Gang leaders and Senior warders. The prison is for non-violent offenders. A batch of new Prisoners has arrived, each sentenced to four years. Everyone will meet in pairs, including meeting their own colleagues.

Before the meetings, the new Prisoners must decide individually and privately whether their behaviour will be basically in support of the Gang leaders or the Senior warders (no other choice is allowed). They must write their decision on their Personal choice sheet and hand it to the facilitator. The choices will be revealed only at the beginning of the debriefing. The decision can be either entirely hypothetical for the purpose of the simulation or what the participant would probably do in that position. The expected effects of the choices are:

* basic support for Gang leaders – easy life among Prisoners and release on parole in three years
* basic support for Senior warders – uneasy life among Prisoners, but release on parole in two years.

Basic support does not mean extreme support, such as participating in a riot or becoming an informer. Uneasy life among Prisoners does not mean any violence apart from some minor jostling, but there would be suspicion, fewer friendships, perhaps, and personal items might disappear more frequently than would be normal.

At the start of each meeting between a new Prisoner and one of the Gang leaders or Senior warders the new Prisoners must tell the Senior warders that they support the Senior warder and must tell the Gang leaders that they support the Gang leader. No equivocations and don't knows are permitted – it must be a straightforward 'I support you' statement, whether true or false.

After a meeting with a new Prisoner, the Gang leaders and Senior warders must record privately whether they think the Prisoner has been telling the truth about the support. (Don't knows are not allowed.) Apart from the Prisoner's opening statement of support, both sides can say what they like. If the Prisoner asks 'Do you believe me?' the Gang leader or Senior warder could tell the truth, lie or be non-committal.

Gang leaders can meet other Gang leaders, Senior warders can meet Senior warders and new Prisoners can meet other new Prisoners. At such meetings, participants can exchange information (true, false, useful, useless, interesting, uninteresting), but each person is expected to behave in accordance with their own best interests.

Individual progress sheet

The position of Gang leaders, Senior warders and new Prisoners can improve, stay the same or deteriorate as a result of the meetings between them.

The position of the Prisoners depends on whether they can tell the truth convincingly and tell an untruth plausibly.

The position of the Gang leaders and Senior warders depends on whether they can tell truth from falsehood.

The payoff is as follows:

Statement	Gang leader or Senior warder marks it as true (T)	Gang leader or Senior warder marks it as false (F)
It is true	Good for Gang leader or Senior warder Good for Prisoner	Bad for Gang leader or Senior warder Bad for Prisoner
It is false	Bad for Gang leader or Senior warder Good for Prisoner	Good for Gang leader or Senior warder Bad for Prisoner

Prisoners

If a Prisoner obtains twice as many good results as bad results, the Prisoner has an easy life and is released in two years.

If a Prisoner obtains twice as many bad results as good results, the Prisoner has an uneasy life and is released in three years.

Gang leaders and Senior warders

If a Gang leader or Senior warder obtains more than twice as many good results as bad results, the Gang leader or Senior warder is promoted to Senior gang leader or Chief warder.

If a Gang leader or Senior warder obtains more than twice as many bad results as good results, the Gang leader or Senior warder is demoted to ordinary Prisoner or ordinary Warder.

Personal choice sheet

Name of prisoner: _____

                                             Senior warders   Gang leaders

In my behaviour I shall give basic support to: ☐   ☐

(Tick one box only and hand form to facilitator)

Personal choice sheet

Name of prisoner: _____

                                             Senior warders   Gang leaders

In my behaviour I shall give basic support to: ☐   ☐

(Tick one box only and hand form to facilitator)

Personal choice sheet

Name of prisoner: _____

                                             Senior warders   Gang leaders

In my behaviour I shall give basic support to: ☐   ☐

(Tick one box only and hand form to facilitator)

Personal choice sheet

Name of prisoner: _____

                                             Senior warders   Gang leaders

In my behaviour I shall give basic support to: ☐   ☐

(Tick one box only and hand form to facilitator)

Senior warder's record sheet

Prisoners	Claim to support Senior warder		Any comments
	True	False	

Gang leaders' record sheet

Prisoners	Claim to support Gang leader		Any comments
	True	False	

Results sheet

Prisoner's choice

Senior warders	Gang leaders	Assessed by Senior warders						Assessed by Gang leaders					Scores (no. of Ts)

Prisoner	Prisoner	Prisoner	Prisoner
Name:	Name:	Name:	Name:
....	....	....	....

Gang leader

Name: ....

Gang leader

Name: ....

Senior warder

Name: _____

Senior warder

Name: _____

48 *Same Again Wine Co.*

Description
This is a simulation about a wine company that recruited staff on the basis of compatibility with existing members of staff and, as a result, faces potential problems regarding race and gender.

Objectives
To enhance the skills of planning within the context of gender and race.

Time and numbers
With small numbers, the event might last for half an hour. If there are several events run in parallel, more time will be needed in the debriefing for explanations, comparisons and comments and then the event could take between an hour and an hour and a half. The minimum number is probably three. There is no maximum number.

Resources
* Briefing sheet – one copy for each participant.
* Report – one copy for each participant.
* Recommendation sheet – one copy for each group, plus spares.
* Scrap paper.

Method
1 If there are more than six participants, mark the Briefing sheets to divide the participants into separate parallel events.

2 Separate the groups as far apart as possible. Hand out the copies of the Report, one to each participant.

3 Hand out the Recommendation sheets, one copy for each group, plus some spares.

4 Set a deadline for the completion of the Recommendation sheets.

5 Retrieve the Briefing sheets and make scrap paper available.

Debriefing
If there were several parallel events, it could be a good idea for each group to debrief themselves and then announce their findings at a joint meeting.

To what extent did the teams plan anything, as distinct from holding an inquest on the present situation at the Company? Did they decide whether to sack people? Did they decide to move staff between departments? Did they change the recruitment policy and, if so, did they abolish the voting system? How many teams included consultation with existing staff as part of their recommendations?

On the race/gender issues, did they feel that the owners had been discriminatory in setting up the recruitment system? Did they think that the result was discriminatory as each department's choice of 'sameness' had excluded a different group?

Did some teams produce Recommendation sheets that consisted mainly of aims, whereas other teams recommended concrete plans? Did they attach anything to the Recommendation sheets – a draft plan, a report, an announcement, a notice, a draft news announcement or a timetable for action? Did they produce anything in writing – jottings, minutes – for their own use?

This is a simulation about a wine company that had recruited staff on the basis of their compatibility with existing employees and, as a result, there are potential problems regarding race and gender.

The husband and wife who were the original owners have sold their business, the Same Again Wine Co., to a conglomerate. You are members of the conglomerate team that has come into the Company on a temporary basis to look at management policy and recruitment policy. You will have a Report on the facts of the situation that was drawn up a week ago by an investigator of the conglomerate. What the Report does not say, but what you know already, is that:

* the policy of the conglomerate is to allow companies considerable autonomy to run themselves and not to impose some form of central control or conformity
* recommendations are only rarely turned down by Headquarters and conglomerate teams are expected to take decisions, not shelve issues or pass them back to Headquarters for a decision
* if the recommendations are accepted, the team will have up to three months to inaugurate the changes, after which it will return to Headquarters.

You have a completely free hand and can take any decision or make any plans you wish, but the bottom line is that your decisions will be expected to be in the long-term interests of the Company and its profitability to the conglomerate. If you feel that any other facts are needed before coming to final decisions, it is up to you to spell out your position on the Recommendation sheet. You can, in addition, draft any document you think might be appropriate.

Report from Investigator McMartin

The Same Again Wine Co. started 20 years ago and was run by a husband and wife team as a family business. The order books and the accounts confirm the view that the Company is on a sound financial footing and is likely to expand its markets still further.

The previous owners' main desire was to have a harmonious staff in each of the three departments – Production, Sales and Finance – that worked very much on their own. The owners allowed every member of a Department to meet candidates who were applying for jobs in that Department and to vote on which ones to choose. As the staff knew that the aim of the owners was to produce harmony, they tended to vote for people like themselves – same sex, same race, same interests. Originally there was only a handful of staff in each Department, but, as the Company grew in size, the difference between employees in one Department and another became more noticeable.

No members of the Accounts Department are male.

No members of the Sales Department are female.

No members of the Production Department belong to an ethnic minority.

The existing staff all wish to keep their jobs and they all seem to be well motivated and their work is commendable. Most of them seem to be either unaware or dismissive of the possibility of future complaints about sexism or ethnic discrimination. There are no signs that any complaints will arise from the staff themselves. I gather that during the last year one or two customers and suppliers who visited the Company expressed surprise that all Accounts staff are female, all Sales staff are male and all Production staff are white. However, none of the visitors made any complaints about this.

Recommendation sheet

Name of company ....

Name of team members ....

Recommendations

_____

_____

_____

_____

_____

_____

_____

_____

_____

_____

_____

_____

_____

Note: Examples or draft documents may be attached to this form.